I0748464

Eight Scandinavian Novelists

Eight Scandinavian Novelists

CRITICISM AND REVIEWS IN ENGLISH

COMPILED BY JOHN BUDD

GREENWOOD PRESS
Westport, Connecticut • London, England

Library of Congress Cataloging in Publication Data

Budd, John, 1953-
Eight Scandinavian novelists.

Includes index.
1. Scandinavian fiction—20th century—History and criticism—Bibliography. 2. Scandinavian fiction—19th century—History and criticism—Bibliography.
I. Title.
Z2559.F52B82 [PT7083] 839'.5 80-24895
ISBN 0-313-22869-8 (lib. bdg.)

Library of Congress Catalog Card Number: 80-24895
ISBN: 0-313-22869-8

First published in 1981

Greenwood Press
A division of Congressional Information Service, Inc.
88 Post Road West, Westport, Connecticut 06881

Printed in the United States of America

10 9 8 7 6 5 4 3 2 1

CONTENTS

PREFACE

This bibliography provides scholars with access to secondary research materials on selected Scandinavian novelists. The citations are restricted to materials in English, since no existing bibliography covers criticism and reviews in English. There are compilations, however, of works on some of these writers in their native languages, usually Swedish and Norwegian.

Of the eight authors included, five have been recipients of the Nobel Prize in literature. Scholarly interest in these writers continues, and one of the goals of this bibliography is to facilitate the efforts of researchers in this country. The authors represented here are some of the major writers of fiction of this century and, in several instances, immediate predecessors of twentieth-century writers who have had a pronounced influence on those who followed them.

Preceding the bibliography section for each author is a brief biographical sketch of that person. The entries for each author are divided first into general works on the writings of the individual, and subdivided according to whether they appear in books, dissertations, chapters and materials in books, or critical articles. The second section, book reviews, is arranged alphabetically by the individual work discussed in the reviews.

Each entry is numbered, and this bibliography includes an index to the authors of the criticism and reviews that refers to the entry numbers. The entries are selectively annotated. Some citations require no annotation, since they contain material similar to that found in other critical judgments. In the case of book reviews, only a relatively small number are annotated. These represent the cross section of reviewers' assessments.

The sources used in the compilation of this bibliography are numerous and varied. What follows is only a partial list of sources consulted.

PARTIAL LIST OF SOURCES CONSULTED

Abstracts of English Studies
Arts and Humanities Citation Index
Book Review Digest
Book Review Index
Comprehensive Index to Little Magazines, 1890-1970
Comprehensive Dissertation Index, 1861-1972, and supplements
Cumulative Book Index
Current Book Review Citations
Essay and General Literature Index
Humanities Index
  preceded by *Social Sciences and Humanities Index*
  preceded by *International Index*
Index to Book Reviews in the Humanities
Kearney, E. I. and L. S. Fitzgerald. *The Continental Novel: A Checklist of Criticism in English, 1900-1966*. Metuchen, N.J.: Scarecrow, 1968.
MLA International Bibliography
Magazine Index
National Library Service Cumulative Book Review Index, 1905-1975
National Union Catalog
Nineteenth Century Readers Guide to Periodical Literature
Poole's Index to Periodical Literature
Readers Guide to Periodical Literature

Eight Scandinavian Novelists

☙ JONAS LIE ❧
1833-1908

Jonas Lie was born on November 6, 1833, at Hokksund. His father, a public official, traveled a great deal while Lie was a youngster. When Jonas was five the family moved to Tromsø in the far north of Norway. The boy was deeply affected by the far northern winters and summers. He was drawn to the harbors and was fascinated by the criminal element. At the age of thirteen Jonas was sent to the Naval Academy in southern Norway.

Jonas failed to qualify for cadet training due to poor eyesight and stayed at the academy at Fredricksvern only six months. During this time he lived in the home of the commodore. This instance returned in his writing. When he returned to Norway from Paris in 1905 he settled in Fredricksvern and one of his novels, The Commodore's Daughters, is influenced by his stay at the academy.

From Fredricksvern he moved to Bergen (where his family had recently taken up residence) and was enrolled at the Cathedral School there. After this he studied law for several years. In 1859 he began to practice as a lawyer.

At this time he also wrote poetry and contributed articles to several papers. From 1861 to 1864 he published Illustreret Nyhedsblad, an important critical review. During the 1860s Norway experienced economic problems and Lie and his wife, Thomasine, had to move to Christiania, where Lie returned to journalism and also taught for a while.

Jonas Lie made his literary debut in 1870 and continued to write until his death in 1908. His first published novel was The Visionary, which was later translated into English. This novel was inspired by the years Lie spent in northern Norway. The story deals with a young man who is endowed with "second sight," an inheritance from his mother. The mother goes insane when she finds out about her son's "curse."

In The Visionary, particularly in sections of "David Holst's Memoirs," Lie takes the opportunity to present his impression of the northland. Lie uses a very realistic style to graphically depict life in Nordland. Through his protagonist he gives a portrayal of the vast mood swings that coincide with the extreme seasonal differences. Lie, however, does not allow his novel to degenerate into an ethnic or regional piece. The novel's center is imbued with universal themes that neither time nor place can limit.

In the 1880s Jonas Lie turned his interest somewhat from the region and began to view modern society with a critical eye. One of the reasons for Lie's broadened consciousness was simple: travel. In 1878 he traveled extensively throughout Germany with stops in Stuttgart, Dresden, and Homburg. In 1882 he took up residence in Paris. He spent most of his time in France until his return to Norway and Fredricksvern. The result of this travel was a cosmopolitan view added to themes that sprung from his childhood and his homeland.

One of the products of this period of Lie's life was the novel Livsslaven, which can be translated as The Slave of Life or One of Life's Slaves. This novel has a social focus that coincides with Lie's blossoming awareness of the modern world. It is not a novel that belongs to any particular class, however. Lie's attention is turned to society as a whole. Though Lie had strong feelings about this particular subject, he did not sentimentalize, nor did he propagandize. Rather, he wrote a psychological novel that simultaneously examines individuals and types.

In The Family at Gilje Lie presented some cultural history of Norway. He used memory as a tool to look back on his own childhood and Norwegian life as it once was. It is a critical view of the past, but a view that is tempered by an affinity Lie had with the bygone days. Perhaps it was the traveling Lie did as a youth that is responsible for his attachment to the past.

Dealing with the past to express views of the human condition was not in vogue at the time that Lie wrote The Family at Gilje. The public paid more attention to the realism of Ibsen. Lie's work may have had a bit more optimism in it. There was an implication of the possibility of a better future in The Family at Gilje. In this way it differed from his earlier writing and the writing of many of his contemporaries.

With a later novel, Niobe, Lie turned his attention to classical tragedy. At the time of the writing, Lie was reading Greek tragedy, so the inspiration for the novel is clear. Niobe represents an artistic attempt on the part of Lie to transfer classical tragedy to the medium of the novel. In structure it closely resembles tragedy. As a modernist, though, Lie injects the tragedy with the trivial, the commonplace. The result is a skeptical and rather conservative novel.

During his lifetime Jonas Lie was somewhat popular in his native Norway and in Scandinavia. He was also read in England, America, Germany, Japan, and other countries. The lack of controversy over his work that may have been at least partly responsible for his early popularity may have also led to his neglect during the first part of the twentieth century.

Many of Lie's contemporaries read his work, and he was especially hailed by young naturalist writers. Of primary interest is Lie's influence on Scandinavian writers who followed him. It has been frequently noted that August Strindberg owed a great debt to Lie and that Knut Hamsun, whose novels show a marked difference from Lie's, also was influenced by his predecessor.

Lie's works demonstrate the admixture of spiritualism and naturalism that became the rule by which he lived. He endeavored to create a work of art that conveyed an accurate portrayal of existence itself. In doing so he experimented with fictional form. His art became his salvation, a means of combining the spiritual with the natural in his own life. He also managed in many ways to combine an impressionistic quality with the realistic novel. The result was a unique form, peculiar to his fiction.

Despite a number of setbacks in his life (some financial), Lie continued his pursuit of art as moral consciousness. He received some government aid to continue with his writing and, in 1904, shortly before he died, he was honored with the Grand Cross of the Order of Saint Olav.

MAJOR WORKS IN ENGLISH

The Commodore's Daughters. Trans. by H. L. Braekstad and Gertrude Hughes. New York: United States Book Co., 1895.

The Family at Gilje. Trans. by Coffin Eastman. Garden City, N. Y.: Doubleday, 1923.

Niobe. Trans. by H. L. Braekstad. New York: G. H. Richmond, 1898.

One of Life's Slaves. Trans. by Jesse Muir. London: Hodder Brothers, 1895.

The Visionary. Trans. by Jesse Muir. London: Hodder Brothers, 1894.

Bibliography

BOOKS

1. Lynstad, Sverre. Jonas Lie. Boston: Twayne Publishers, 1977.

Lynstad's biography of Lie is largely critical, examining Lie's major works in the context of his own life and times. Lynstad also points out the considerable influence of Lie and his work, particularly on other Scandinavian writers.

CHAPTERS AND MATERIALS IN BOOKS

2. Bach, Giovanni. "Norwegian Literature." In A History of the Scandinavian Literatures. Trans. and ed. Frederika Blankner. New York: Dial, 1938, pp. 49-50.

In his history, Bach devotes a small bit of attention to Lie. He gives like notice to Garborg, Lagerlöf, Lagerkvist, Hamsun, Laxness, and Undset.

3. Boyesen, Hjalmar H. "Jonas Lie." In Essays on Scandinavian Literature. New York: Scribner's, 1895, pp. 121-51.

Boyesen notes the conflict between Lie's staid righteousness and a sort of wanderlust. This conflict, which may have been precipitated by his parents' backgrounds, is manifest in virtually all of his works. Other influences, primarily economic, are also noted.

4. Cortissoz, Royal. "Jonas Lie." In American Academy of Arts and Letters. Commemorative Tributes of the Academy, 1905-1941. New York: The Academy, 1942, pp. 397-9.

5. ________. "Jonas Lie." In American Academy of Arts and Letters. Commemorative Tributes to Gillette and Howard. New York: The Academy, 1940, pp. 23-7.

6. Cunliffe, J. W., et. al., eds. "Jonas Lie." In vol. 10 of Columbia University Course in Literature Based on the World's Best Literature. New York: Columbia University Press, 1928-1929, pp. 252-3.

7. Cunliffe, J. W. and A. H. Thorndike, eds. "Jonas Lie." In vol 15 of The Warner Library. New York: U.S. Publications Associations, 1917, pp. 9048-50.

8. Downs, Brian Westerdale. "Elster and Lie." In Modern Norwegian Literature, 1860-1918. Cambridge, Eng.: Cambridge University Press, 1966, pp. 65-79.

Downs refers to Lie as "Norway's great 'Victorian' novelist." He refers to Lie as the first Norwegian novelist to explore many aspects of the life of modern Norway.

9. Gustafson, Alrik. "Impressionistic Realism; Jonas Lie." In Six Scandinavian Novelists. New York: Princeton University Press, 1940, pp. 25-72.

Gustafson studies Lie's life and writings, recognizing the traditionalism mixed with tempered progress of his works. Gustafson also notes the importance of the international attention Lie received and the fact that he was Scandinavia's first really important novelist.

10. McFarlane, James W. "Jonas Lie." In Ibsen and the Temper of Norwegian Literature. London: Oxford University Press, 1960, pp. 97-103.

11. Wergeland, Agnes M. "Second-Sight in Norse Literature." In Leaders in Norway and Other Essays. Ed. Katherina Merrill. Menasha, Wis.: Banta Publications, 1916, pp. 139-45.

CRITICAL ARTICLES

12. Berry, R. V. S. "Jonas Lie: The Man and His Art." American Magazine of Art 16 (February, 1925), 58-66.

13. Bjornson, Bjornstjerne. "Modern Norwegian Literature, II." Forum 21 (June, 1896), 398-413.

14. Brown, James Wesley. "Charles Dickens and Norwegian Belle-Lettres in the Nineteenth Century." Edda, No. 2 (1970), 65-84.

15. Downs, Brian Westerdale. "Anglo-Norwegian Literary Relations, 1867-1900." Modern Language Review 47 (October, 1952), 449-94.
In his brief section on Lie, Downs states that more of Lie's works could be translated into English, though he says that Lie is not a "great creative artist."

16. "Exhibition." American-Scandinavian Review 26 (June, 1938), 178.

17. "Jonas Lie." Literary World 13, 114.

18. Larsen, Hanna Astrup. "Jonas Lie, 1933-1909 [sic] ." American-Scandinavian Review 21 (1933), 461-71.

19. Rose, B. "America as Paradise." Partisan Review 44 (1977), 62-70.

20. Wiehr, J. "Women Characters of Jonas Lie." Journal of English and Germanic Philology 28 (January-April, 1929), 244-62.
Wiehr notes Lie somewhat alienated both the traditional, conventional women and the women's rights advocates, though his women characters are often stronger in many ways than the men.

BOOK REVIEWS

Commodore's Daughter

21. "Commodore's Daughter." Athenaeum, 21 May 1892, p. 663.

Family at Gilje

22. "Family at Gilje." New York Times Book Review, 18 November 1923, p. 9.
The reviewer says that there is a "superb naturalness" of the story. The plot and characterizations are totally devoid of artificiality.

23. "Family at Gilje." Wisconsin Library Bulletin 19 (December, 1923), 508.

Niobe

24. "Niobe." Nation, 11 May 1899, p. 358.

One of Life's Slaves

25. "One of Life's Slaves." Athenaeum, 26 September 1896, p. 415.

26. "One of Life's Slaves." Westminster Review 143 (April, 1895), 473.

Visionary

27. "Visionary." Athenaeum, 14 April 1894, p. 473.

ARNE GARBORG
1851-1924

Arne Garborg was born on his family farm south of Stravenger in southwestern Norway on January 25, 1851. His family was not wealthy, but the land had belonged to the Garborgs for many years and Arne's father was a rather prominent man in that locale. Eivind Garborg, Arne's father, went through a period of religious crisis that made him exceedingly somber. This period had a pronounced effect on the Garborg family, since the father forbade the children to read books. Eivind Garborg's fanaticism continued to the extent that he committed suicide in 1870.

Arne left the farm, but a nagging feeling of guilt remained with him for disrupting the family. At first he became a teacher, but he found that the profession was not to his liking. Then he became the editor of a teachers' journal. Shortly after beginning this enterprise he added a rather liberal newspaper to his editorial duties. In spite of the paper's liberal nature, Garborg's own articles were religiously and politically conservative.

Garborg's earliest writing experiences were in poetry. His first poem appeared in a Stravenger newspaper in 1870 under the pseudonym "Alf Buestreng." He moved to Christiania and studied at the university. While a student Garborg supported himself with journalistic endeavors. He would write somewhat inflammatory articles on pertinent topics of the day. In the capitol city he became interested in and influenced by modern ideas. He joined a naturalist movement that stressed a national language. For five years, from 1877 to 1882, Garborg edited an agrarian paper that catered to naturalist ideas.

His studies led him to evolution, positivism, and modern literature. These studies greatly influenced him and led to his becoming an atheistic naturalist. Some of his early writing was at least partly autobiographical. He wrote about young men who had forsaken their peasant upbringing and who had transplanted themselves in the city. Criticism of the popular peasant romanticism was included in his writing of this period.

In 1879 Garborg was employed by the government and worked in the state auditor's office. Even while he was employed by the government he continued his criticism of social, political, religious, and sexual mores. In 1886 he published his naturalistic novel <u>Menfolk</u>. The novel deals frankly with sexual and moral issues in a way that was displeasing to established society. The publication of the book resulted in the loss of his government job as an auditor.

Garborg married Karen Hulda Bergersen in 1887. She shared many of his radical ideas and became a writer herself. He and his wife moved away from the city to a cottage in the Dovre mountains of central Norway. There his only son was born. Garborg continued to write about societal ills, but he also wrote about the beauty of nature.

The negativism of the atheistic ideology became less attractive to Garborg in the 1890s. He was also disillusioned by promiscuity that masqueraded itself as free love. He was greatly influenced at this time by the neo-romantic writing of the 1890s. He read Nietzche and Tolstoy and their ideas became evident in his books. Tired Men, an epistolary novel published in 1891, portrays a modern mind that developed without the benefit of religion or traditional morality. It was highly critical of espousing new ideas while completely tossing out the old.

Garborg remained an agnostic, even after he realized the importance and validity of traditional ideas. He was never able to embrace dogmatic religion as had been so fanatically preached by his father, but he was able to develop a kind of undogmatic religion. This religion was based in part on his reading of the Gospels and on the spirit of love expressed by the evangelists. This attitude of his is voiced literally in his novel Peace. His childhood and memories of his father provided a basis for the book. He continued the story of the characters he introduced in Peace in later novels that have not been translated.

In his later years he became less active as a writer, but he became a serious student of Jonas Lie. His works embody both the naturalism of many Scandinavian writers and the reaction to overemphasis on modern ideas that is characteristic of others. Unfortunately, little of his work has been translated into English. He died of pneumonia on January 14, 1924.

MAJOR WORKS IN ENGLISH

Peace. Trans. by Phillips Dean Carleton. New York: American-Scandinavian Foundation, W. W. Norton, 1929.

DISSERTATIONS

28. Lillehei, Ingebrigt Larsen. "A Study in the Language and the Main Ideas of Arne Garborg's Works." Diss. University of Illinois at Urbana-Champaign, 1914.

CHAPTERS AND MATERIALS IN BOOKS

29. Bach, Giovanni. "Norwegian Literature." In A History of the Scandinavian Literatures. Trans. and ed. Frederika Blankner. New York: Dial, 1938, pp. 50-3.

30. Cunliffe, J. W. and A. H. Thorndike, eds. "Arne Garborg." In vol. 10 of The Warner Library. New York: U.S. Publications Association, 1917, pp. 6185-7.

31. Downs, Brian Westerdale. "Garborg and Other Landsmaal Authors of His Time." In Modern Norwegian Literature, 1860-1918. Cambridge, Eng.: Cambridge University Press, 1966, pp. 99-115.
In discussing Garborg, Downs notes his facility with naturalistic reality, especially in the novel Peace. This, along with his Christiania novels, displays his versatility while remaining in a narrow geographical area.

CRITICAL ARTICLES

32. Larsen, Hanna Astrup. "Arne Garborg." American-Scandinavian Review 12 (May, 1924), 274-88.

33. Sjavik, J. "From Little Daniel to Student Braut." Scandinavian Studies 50 (1978), 439-41.

BOOK REVIEWS

Peace

34. Basinger, A. L. "Peace." New York Herald-Tribune Books, 15 December 1929, p. 5.

35. Bell, Lisle. "Peace." New York Herald-Tribune Books, 27 April 1930, p. 10.

36. Hutchison, Percy. "Peace." New York Times Book Review, 29 December 1929, p. 8.
    Hutchison recognizes the power of Garborg's narrative, particularly the religious aspects of the novel, but he says that the average American reader may find Peace distasteful.

37. "Peace." Booklist 26(July, 1930), 397.

38. "Peace." Nation, 27 August 1930, p. 229.
    This reviewer says that Peace portrays the phenomenon of religious monomania better than any book yet written. He adds that Garborg "has wrung beauty and majesty as the background for the tragedy."

39. "Peace." New Statesman, 31 May 1930, p. 247.

40. "Peace." Pittsburgh Monthly Bulletin 35(March, 1930), 23.

41. "Peace." Saturday Review of Literature, 29 March 1930, p. 880.

42. "Peace." Springfield Republican, 20 July 1930, p. 5e.

43. "Peace." The Times (London) Literary Supplement, 24 July 1930, p. 603.

44. Snow, Francis. "Peace." Current History Magazine of the New York Times 31(March, 1930), 1046.
    Snow finds the novel too realistic to embody any spiritual ideals. He says it is "stark and grim."

45. Tomlinson, K. C. "Peace." Nation and Athenaeum, 12 July 1930, p. 477.

SELMA LAGERLÖF
1858-1940

Selma Otilia Lovisa Lagerlöf was born in Värmland on November 20, 1858. Unfortunately, before she turned four years old she was stricken with infantile paralysis. In an effort to cure her, the Lagerlöf family lived for a brief time in Strömstad in western Sweden in the summer of 1863. This interlude was one of happiness for the Lagerlöfs, with new friendships made. Selma regained her ability to walk, though she was to carry a limp for the rest of her life. This journey to Strömstad made an indelible impression on Selma and she wrote in an autobiography that she remembered her family best as they were at the time.

During her childhood Selma paid close attention to the folktales told her. The oral narratives of her aunt, Otiliana Lagerlöf, were of particular interest to the young Selma and had a profound effect on her writing. The influence is obvious in sections of The Story of Gösta Berling in which many childhood impressions are related. In her imagination, Selma Lagerlöf frequently returned to Mårbacka, the family mansion, and to the folktales that were a large part of her education.

Selma's father died when she was in her early twenties and financial difficulties for the Lagerlöf family ensued. As a result of the difficulties the family lost Mårbacka. Selma had been preparing for the teaching profession and took a position in Landskrona in northern Sweden. This area, along with Värmland, became a major source and background for much of her writing. She had a strong feeling for the land and the people of the land and seldom strayed from these areas, either physically or in her writing.

While a teacher she began writing and occasionally published poetry, but she met with no great success until the appearance of The Story of Gösta Berling in 1891. Several critics have pointed out that Lagerlöf's style in this book was greatly influenced by her reading of Carlyle, especially of Heroes and Hero Worship. The first five chapters of her novel won her a prize from the magazine Idun. It marked the first recognition of her writing talents.

She continued to write and in 1895 was awarded a traveling fellowship and left the profession of teaching. She took advantage of the fellowship and went to Italy to study the literature of that country. After a brief stay there, and despite her lameness, she traveled across most of Europe and the Palestinian countryside. When she returned to Sweden she bought a house in Falun with some of the money earned by her writing and lived there with her mother and aunt.

Her Palestinian journey made such an impression on her that she wrote a novel entitled Jerusalem, which was originally published in two volumes in 1901 and 1902. Jerusalem appeared in English in 1915 and The Holy City—Jerusalem II was published in 1918. These works were prompted by her observation of the emigration of a number of Swedish families (at the urging of a Chicago revivalist who exerted his influence over people in Sweden and Swedish families who had previously emigrated to America) to Jerusalem. Some Swedish-Americans had founded a colony there and more Swedes joined them. During her excursion to the Holy Land Lagerlöf visited this colony and found a place for it in her writing.

In 1904 she was awarded the gold medal of the Swedish Academy. In 1914 she was elected the first woman member of the Academy, the group responsible for the selection of Nobel Prize recipients. Prior to her election to the Academy, in 1909 she was awarded the Nobel Prize in literature, the first woman and the first Swede to be so honored. With the money that accompanied the Nobel Prize she bought back Mårbacka and remodeled it. She lived there until her death.

Her style grew away from that of Carlyle and eventually settled into one of simplicity, which befitted the themes of her stories. The literary style of her later writing has often been likened to Hans Christian Andersen's and strongly resembles that of the folktales told to her in her childhood. The simplicity betrays a kind of optimistic naiveté that was shaken only by the First World War and the threat of another war at the time of her death.

Her simplicity was the major criticism of later readers. The lack of controversy, of social awareness, seemed to many to have a detrimental effect on her writing. She never allowed political, social, or religious views to overshadow the story she was trying to tell. It is this very simplicity, though, that accounts for her popularity. The primitive quality of her tales that spring from the Swedish soil and the people who work that soil was the same quality inherent in the tales she heard in her youth. She was able to convey with fascinating results legends and sagas that combined the ancient world of the epics with the modern world.

During her lifetime her popularity became so great that millions purchased her books and many of her novels were adapted to the screen. For at least forty-five years after its release, _The Story of Gösta Berling_ was the most popular novel in Sweden. Her works have been translated into more than thirty languages. By 1930 nearly two million copies of her books had been sold in her native Sweden alone. The critical concensus is that _Jerusalem_ and _The Story of_

Gösta Berling are her finest works and that these and some of her shorter novels have insured Selma Lagerlöf's place in world literature.

MAJOR WORKS IN ENGLISH

Charlotte Löwenskold. Trans. by Velma Swanston Howard. Garden City, N. Y.: Doubleday, 1927.

Christ Legends. Trans. by Velma Swanston Howard. New York: Holt, Rinehart and Winston, 1908.

The Emperor of Portugalia. Trans. by Velma Swanston Howard. Garden City, N. Y.: Doubleday, 1916.

Further Adventures of Nils. Trans. by Velma Swanston Howard. Garden City, N. Y.: Doubleday, 1911.

The General's Ring. Trans. by Francesca Martin. Garden City, N. Y.: Doubleday, 1928.

The Girl from Marsh Croft. Trans. by Velma Swanston Howard. Boston: Little, Brown, 1910.

The Holy City—Jerusalem II. Trans. by Velma Swanston Howard. Garden City, N. Y.: Doubleday, 1918.

Jerusalem. Trans. by Velma Swanston Howard, Garden City, N. Y.: Doubleday, 1915.

Liliecrona's Home. Trans. by Anna Barwell. New York: Dutton, 1914.

Miracles of Antichrist. Trans. by Selma Ahlström Trotz. New York: Lovell, 1899.

The Outcast. Trans. by W. Worster. Garden City, N. Y.: Doubleday, 1922.

Queens of Küngahalla and Other Sketches. Trans. by C. Field. London: T. W. Laurie, 1930.

The Ring of the Löwenskolds. Trans. by Velma Swanston Howard. Garden City, N. Y.: Doubleday, 1931.

The Story of Gösta Berling. Trans. by Pauline Bancroft Flach. Boston: Little, Brown, 1898.
Gösta Berling's Saga. Trans. by Velma Swanston Howard. New York: American-Scandinavian Foundation, 1919.

The Treasure. Trans. by Arthur G. Chater. Garden City, N. Y.: Doubleday, 1925.

The Wonderful Adventures of Nils. Trans. by Velma Swanston Howard. Garden City, N. Y.: Doubleday, 1907.
The Wonderful Adventures of Nils. Trans. by Richard E. Oldenburg. Garden City, N. Y.: Doubleday, 1967.

BOOKS

46. Berendsohn, Walter Arthur. Selma Lagerlöf; Her Life and Work. Adapted from the German by George F. Timpson. Port Washington, N. Y.: Kennikat Press, 1968.

47. Larsen, Hanna Astrup. Selma Lagerlöf. Garden City, N. Y.: Doubleday, 1936.
This brief biography is largely factual, but it does present many aspects of Lagerlöf's life which had influence on her writing. Larsen also relates the evolution of many of Lagerlöf's major works, recognizing her tremendous popular appeal, not just in Sweden, but worldwide.

48. Maule, H. F. Selma Lagerlöf: The Woman, Her Work, Her Message. Garden City, N. Y.: Doubleday, 1917.

DISSERTATIONS

49. Nelson, Anne Theodora. "The Critical Reception of Selma Lagerlöf in France." Diss. Northwestern University, 1962.

CHAPTERS AND MATERIALS IN BOOKS

50. Allen, W. Gore. "The Protestants: Selma Lagerlöf." In Renaissance in the North. New York: Sheed & Ward, 1946, pp. 72-86.
Allen concentrates on Lagerlöf's religious views, particularly Lutheran moralism as displayed in her novels. He focuses on Gösta Berling's Saga (The Story of Gösta Berling) and the circumstances by which she came to be a writer.

51. Bach, Giovanni. "Swedish Literature." In A History of the Scandinavian Literature. Trans. and ed. Frederika Blankner. New York: Dial, 1938, pp. 136-8.

52. Bjorkman, Edwin August. "Story of Selma Lagerlöf." In Voices of Tomorrow: Critical Essays of the New Spirit in Literature. New York: Kennerly, 1913, pp. 139-53.

Bjorkman sees Lagerlöf's writing as a synthesis of romanticism and naturalism. He also sees this synthesis as a product of the time. The bulk of his section on Lagerlöf is biographical.

53. Brewster, D. "Selma Lagerlöf." In vol. 10 of The Columbia University Course in Literature. Ed. J. W. Cunliffe, et. al. New York: Columbia University Press, 1928-1929, pp. 182-5.

54. Cooper, Anice Page. "Selma Lagerlöf." In Authors and Others. Garden City, N. Y.: Doubleday, Page, 1927, pp. 81-95.

55. Cunliffe, J. W. and A. H. Thorndike, eds. "Selma Lagerlöf." In vol. 14 of The Warner Library. New York: U.S. Publications Association, 1917, pp. 8800a-8800d.

56. Gustafson, Alrik. "Saga and Legend of a Province; Selma Lagerlöf." In Six Scandinavian Novelists. New York: Princeton University Press, 1940, pp. 177-225.

Gustafson recognizes that Lagerlöf cannot be considered without also considering her homeland. The influence of her family and her home was the single most important factor in the development of her fiction. She uses the legends and traditions freely in her storytelling.

57. Hesse, Hermann. "Selma Lagerlöf." In My Belief: Essays on Life and Art. Ed. and with intro. by Theodore Ziolkowski. Trans. Denver Lindley with two essays trans. by Ralph Manheim. New York: Farrar, Straus, Giroux, 1979, pp. 317-23.

Hesse remarks that Lagerlöf is not a literary genius and that there are flaws in her works, but he also states that she has an almost magnetic appeal. He points out the differences between her writing and that of other modern Swedish authors.

58. Kirkland, Winifred Margaretta and Frances Kirkland. "Selma Lagerlöf, Who Listened and Remembered." In Girls Who Became Writers. New York: Harper's, 1933, pp. 13-25.

59. Marble, Mrs. Annie Russell. "Selma Lagerlöf--Swedish Realist and Idealist." In Nobel Prize Winners in Literature, 1901-1931. New York: Appleton-Century, 1932, pp. 104-23.
Marble presents a brief biographical sketch of Lagerlöf. She notes especially Lagerlöf's nationalism which shows clearly in her novels.

60. Monroe, Nellie Elizabeth. "Provisional Art in Selma Lagerlöf." In Novel and Society: A Critical Study of the Modern Novel. Chapel Hill, N. C.: University of North Carolina Press, 1941, pp. 88-110.
Monroe concentrates on the simplicity of Lagerlöf's writing and of her characters. Monroe states that this is not necessarily a failing because she is so adept at story-telling. Her naiveté separates her from other modern writers.

CRITICAL ARTICLES

61. Afzelius, Nils. "The Scandalous Selma Lagerlöf." Scandinavica 5 (November, 1966), 91-9.
Afzelius presents a kind of critical history of Lagerlöf's works, particularly Gösta Berling's Saga.

62. Danielson, Larry W. "The Uses of Demonic Folk Tradition in Selma Lagerlöf's Gösta Berling's Saga." Western Folklore 34 (July, 1975), 187-99.
Danielson concentrates upon the romantic aspect of Gösta Berling's Saga, particularly with relation to the Värmland supernatural folk traditions and their incorporation into the character of Sintram.

63. Flinch, O. "Criticism." Outlook, 19 April 1902, pp. 977-80.

64. Johannesson, Eric O. "Isak Dineson and Selma Lagerlöf." Scandinavian Studies 32 (1960), 18-26.
Lagerlöf, a more traditional writer (both in terms of structure and theme), has not been considered by Johannesson as having a great influence on younger Scandinavian writers. Her works are more positive and romantic than most writers of her time.

65. Lagerroth, Erland. "The Narrative Art of Selma Lagerlöf: Two Problems." Scandinavian Studies 33 (February, 1961), 10-7.

Lagerroth looks at the relationship between characters and setting in Lagerlöf's fiction and at what he calls "the poetic machinery of her writing."

66. ________. "Selma Lagerlöf Research, 1900-1964: A Survey and an Orientation." Scandinavian Studies 37 (February, 1965), 1-30.

This survey concerns itself almost entirely with works in Swedish and German.

67. Lagerroth, Ulla-Britta. "The Troll in Man--A Lagerlöf Motif." Scandinavian Studies 40 (February, 1968), 51-60.

Lagerroth studies the use and symbolism of trolls in many of Lagerlöf's stories, concentrating especially on the theme of the changling.

68. Leach, H. G. "Selma Lagerlöf in America." American-Scandinavian Review 16 (December, 1928), 747.

69. Monroe, Elizabeth. "Selma Lagerlöf's Art." American-Scandinavian Review 28 (June, 1940), 143-7.

70. "Novels of Lagerlöf." Living Age 4 January 1902, pp. 8-11.

71. "Passing of Selma Lagerlöf." American-Scandinavian Review 28 (June, 1940), 141-3.

72. Pehrson, Elsa. "Glimpses from the Hidden Workshop of Selma Lagerlöf." American-Scandinavian Review 33 (1945), 41-4.

73. Raphael, Robert. "Gösta Berling of the Lyric Stage." Scandinavian Studies 42 (February, 1970), 31-8.

Raphael's article concerns the transformation of Gösta Berling's Saga into an operatic form.

74. Terras, Victor. "Two Bronze Monarchs." Scandinavian Studies 33 (August, 1961), 150-4.

Terras cites some similarities between The Wonderful Adventures of Nils and Pushkin's poem "The Bronze Horseman."

BOOK REVIEWS

Charlotte Löwensköld

75. Brickell, Herschel. "Charlotte Löwenskold." North American Review 225 (January, 1928), adv.

76. "Charlotte Löwenskold." Boston Transcript, 17 December 1927, p. 9.

77. "Charlotte Löwenskold." New York Times Book Review, 23 October 1927, p. 6.
The reviewer points out some perceived shortcomings: it is out-of-date, it doesn't depict real life, it is not particularly memorable. In spite of this the reviewer finds much to recommend the book.

78. "Charlotte Löwenskold." New York World, 11 December 1927, p. 11m.

79. Mann, D. L. "Charlotte Löwenskold." New York Evening Post, 26 November 1927, p. 13.

80. Matthews, T. S. "Charlotte Löwenskold." New Republic, 4 January 1928, p. 201.

81. Parsons, A. B. "Charlotte Löwenskold." New York Herald-Tribune Books, 23 October 1927, p. 5.
Parsons likens Lagerlöf's novel to Scott's and Cooper's and says that it may be most enjoyed by "high-spirited youth."

Christ Legends

82. "Christ Legends." New York Times Saturday Review, 5 December 1908, p. 745.

83. "Christ Legends." New York Times Saturday Review, 5 December 1908, p. 750.

Emperor of Portugalia

84. "Emperor of Portugallia." Booklist 13 (January, 1917), 176.

85. "Emperor of Portugallia." Catholic World 104 (February, 1917), 697.
This reviewer says "the writer's pessimism is revolting," but he finds the characters lifelike.

86. "Emperor of Portugallia." Independent, 25 December 1916, p. 551.

87. "Emperor of Portugallia." Literary Digest, 13 January 1917, p. 83.

88. "Emperor of Portugallia." Nation, 25 January 1917, p. 106.

89. "Emperor of Portugallia." New York Times Book Review, 22 October 1916, p. 438.

90. "Emperor of Portugallia." Outlook, 15 November 1916, p. 616.
The reviewer remarks on the sincerity and simplicity of the telling of the tale which he says is "infinitely tragic."

91. "Emperor of Portugallia." Springfield Republican, 7 January 1917, p. 15.

92. Hale, E. "Emperor of Portugallia." Dial, 30 November 1916, p. 467.

93. Mann, D. L. "Emperor of Portugallia." Boston Transcript, 2 December 1916, p. 6.

94. Tilinghast, Philip. "Emperor of Portugallia." Publishers' Weekly, 9 December 1916, p. 2074.

From a Swedish Homestead

95. "From a Swedish Homestead." Bookman 13 (July, 1901), 500.

Further Adventures of Nils

96. "Further Adventures of Nils." Booklist 8 (December, 1911), 181.

The reviewer states that the novel is "vividly Imagined," but the earlier adventures of Nils should be read first for full appreciation of the work.

97. "Further Adventures of Nils." Review of Reviews 44 (December, 1911), 764.

The General's Ring

98. "The General's Ring." Booklist 25 (October, 1928), 29.

99. "The General's Ring." Cleveland Open Shelf, December 1928, p. 137.

100. "The General's Ring." Independent, 14 April 1928, p. 365.

The reviewer says that it is an engaging story and that Lagerlöf manages to make real her characters and her scenes.

101. "The General's Ring." Nation, 25 April 1928, p. 494.

102. "The General's Ring." New York Evening Post, 24 March 1928, p. 13.

103. "The General's Ring." New York Times Book Review, 22 April 1928, p. 19.

104. "The General's Ring." Pittsburgh Monthly Bulletin 33 (October, 1928), 430.

105. Lohrke, Eugene. "The General's Ring." New York Herald-Tribune Books, 11 March 1928, p. 7.

Girl from the Marsh Croft

106. "Girl from the Marsh Croft." Booklist 6 (June, 1910), 410.

107. "Girl from the Marsh Croft." New York Times Saturday Review, 14 May 1910, p. 273.
The reviewer says that the stories are very good, but, more importantly, they presage a talent which is not yet fully developed.

108. "Girl from the Marsh Croft." Outlook, 30 July 1910, p. 750.

109. "Girl from the Marsh Croft." Review of Reviews 41 (June, 1910), 759.

Holy City--Jerusalem II

110. Bourne, Randolph. "Holy City--Jerusalem II." Dial, 5 September 1918, p. 167.
Bourne notes the ability of Lagerlöf to remain detached while portraying intense interplay among her characters.

111. "Holy City--Jerusalem II." Booklist 14 (July, 1918), 339.

112. "Holy City--Jerusalem II." Cleveland Open Shelf, July 1918, p. 78.

113. "Holy City--Jerusalem II." Literary Digest, 25 May 1918, p. 38.

114. "Holy City--Jerusalem II." Nation, 12 October 1918, p. 427.
The novel fails for this reviewer because of what he sees as the protracted bitterness encompassing the entire novel.

115. "Holy City--Jerusalem II." New York Times Book Review, 14 April 1918, p. 167.

116. "Holy City--Jerusalem II." Springfield Republican, 1 September 1918, p. 13.

117. Mann, D. L. "Holy City--Jerusalem II." Boston Transcript, 6 April 1918, p. 7.

118. Webb, Doris. "Holy City--Jerusalem II." Publishers' Weekly, 20 April 1918, p. 1270.

Jerusalem

119. Cooper, F. T. "Jerusalem." Bookman 42 (November, 1915), 323.

Cooper especially praises the concluding chapter which, he says, has achieved levels of pathos and tragedy that are seldom reached.

120. "Jerusalem." Booklist 12 (December, 1915), 138.

121. "Jerusalem." Boston Transcript, 25 September 1915, p. 7.

122. "Jerusalem." Independent, 8 November 1915, p. 237.

123. "Jerusalem." Literary Digest, 16 October 1915, p. 847.

124. "Jerusalem." Little Review 2 (October, 1915), 40.

125. "Jerusalem." New Republic, 15 November 1915, p. 50.

126. "Jerusalem." New York Times Book Review, 31 October 1915, p. 413.

The reviewer says that the power of this novel lies in the fact that readers can identify completely with the characters. Reviews of Jerusalem are uniformly laudatory.

127. "Jerusalem." Springfield Republican, 28 November 1915, p. 17.

128. Lynd, Robert. "Jerusalem." Publishers' Weekly, 18 September 1915, p. 787.

Legend of the Sacred Image

129. "Legend of the Sacred Image." Boston Transcript, 13 January 1915, p. 22.

130. "Legend of the Sacred Image." Dial, 16 December 1914, p. 509.

Liliecrona's Home

131. Cooper, F. T. "Liliecrona's Home." Bookman 39 (April, 1914), 209.

132. "Liliecrona's Home." Athenaeum, 1 November 1913, p. 494.

    The reviewer notes that this is a short tale with elementary but lifelike characters.

133. "Liliecrona's Home." Booklist 10 (April, 1914) p. 326.

134. "Liliecrona's Home." Boston Transcript, 14 February 1914, p. 6.

135. "Liliecrona's Home." Boston Transcript, 26 March 1914, p. 10.

136. "Liliecrona's Home." Literary Digest, 21 March 1914, p. 626.

137. "Liliecrona's Home." Nation, 5 March 1914, p. 239.

138. "Liliecrona's Home." New Republic, 20 April 1927, p. 257.

139. "Liliecrona's Home." New York Times Book Review, 30 January 1927, p. 9.

140. "Liliecrona's Home." Review of Reviews 99 (May, 1914), 628.

141. "Liliecrona's Home." Spectator, 18 April 1914, p. 654.

142. Rigg, Margaret. "Liliecrona's Home." New York Herald-Tribune Books, 30 January 1927, p. 3.
Rigg says that this novel is inferior to Gosta Berling's Saga. She offers the opinion that perhaps Lagerlof is no longer able to equal the realism of the earlier work. The novel, however, was published some time before 1927.

Miracles of Antichrist

143. "Miracles of Antichrist." Arena 22 (August, 1899), 295-6.

144. "Miracles of Antichrist." Bookman 9 (July, 1899), 474.

145. "Miracles of Antichrist." Bookman (London) 16 (July, 1899), 111.

146. "Miracles of Antichrist." Catholic World, 69 (May, 1899), 272-6.

147. "Miracles of Antichrist." Critic 35 (August, 1899), 766-7.

148. "Miracles of Antichrist." Dial, 1 May 1899, p. 310.

Outcast

149. Burke, B. U. "Outcast." Nation, 21 December 1921, p. 734.

150. Hawthorne, Hidegarde. "Outcast." New York Times Book Review, 12 March 1922, p. 11.

151. Hibbard, C. A. "Outcast." Greensboro (North Carolina) Daily News, 3 September 1922, p. 10.

152. Mann, D. L. "*Outcast*." *Boston Transcript*, 12 April 1922, p. 5.
Mann states that the simplicity of the story and the people in the story give reality to the novel. He is of the opinion that it is her best work as of the time of his writing.

153. "*Outcast*." *Dial* 73 (July, 1922), 112.

154. "*Outcast*." *Dial* 73 (September, 1922), 354.

155. "*Outcast*." *North American Review* 215 (May, 1922), 711.

156. "*Outcast*." *Springfield Republican*, 16 April 1922, p. 13a. Rpt. from *Manchester Guardian*.
The reviewer notes that the tale is somewhat didactic, but it is sincere and is artfully written.

157. "*Outcast*." *Springfield Republican*, 26 June 1922, p. 9a. Rpt. from *Manchester Guardian*.

158. "*Outcast*." *The Times (London) Literary Supplement*, 23 December 1920, p. 875.

159. "*Outcast*." *Wisconsin Library Bulletin* 18 (May, 1922), 133.

160. Porterfield, A. W. "*Outcast*." *Literary Review of the New York Evening Post*, 8 April 1922, p. 560.

161. Rickert, Edith. "*Outcast*." *New Republic*, 12 July 1922, p. 194.
Rickert reviews *Outcast* negatively. She says it is mired in propaganda and Lagerlof's treatment is "kaleidoscopic."

162. Townsend, R. D. "*Outcast*." *Pittsburgh Monthly Bulletin* 27 (November, 1922), 461.

Queens of Küngahalla and Other Sketches

163. "Queens of Küngahalla and Other Sketches." Cleveland Open Shelf, December 1917, p. 132.

164. "Queens of Küngahalla and Other Sketches." The Times (London) Literary Supplement, 15 March 1917, p. 127.
The reviewer praises Lagerlöf's ability to create and make convincing an entire imaginative world, while lending it an air of reality.

Ring of the Löwenskolds

165. Cantwell, Robert. "Ring of the Löwenskolds." New Republic, 25 February 1931, p. 51.

166. Carleton, Philip. "Ring of the Löwenskolds." Saturday Review of Literature, 7 February 1931, p. 580.
Carleton states that the romanticism that adds charm to Lagerlöf's stories also gives them an air of unreality. The characters, though graceful, lack depth.

167. Hansen, Harry. "Ring of the Löwenskolds." New York World, 10 January 1931, p. 11.

168. Mann, D. L. "Ring of the Löwenskolds." Boston Transcript, 31 January 1931, p. 2.

169. Parsons, A. B. "Ring of the Löwenskolds." New York Herald-Tribune Books, 4 January 1931, p. 1.

170. "Ring of the Löwenskolds." Booklist 27 (March, 1931), p. 312.

171. "Ring of the Löwenskolds." Christian Science Monitor, 7 February 1931, p. 10.

172. "Ring of the Löwenskolds." Cleveland Open Shelf, June 1931, p. 94.

173. "Ring of the Löwenskolds." New York Times Book Review, 4 January 1931, p. 4.

174. "Ring of the Löwenskolds." Pittsburgh Monthly Bulletin 36 (February, 1931), 12.

175. "Ring of the Löwenskolds." Pratt Institute Quarterly, Spring 1931, p. 37.

176. "Ring of the Löwenskolds." Springfield Republican, 11 January 1931, p. 7e.

177. Robbins, F. L. "Ring of the Löwenskolds." Outlook and Independent, 7 January 1931, p. 26.
Robbins says that the trilogy makes a smooth transition from folk tale to comedy of manners. Lagerlöf is able to add humor and humanity to the work.

178. Sykes, Gerald. "Ring of the Löwenskolds." Bookman 72 (February, 1931), 632.
Sykes finds Lagerlöf lacking artistically. He acknowledges her skill as a storyteller, but finds her stylistic ability somewhat deficient.

179. Walton, E. L. "Ring of the Löwenskolds." Nation, 11 February 1931, p. 157.

Story of Gösta Berling or Gösta Berling's Saga

180. Bealby, J. T. "Reply to Review of Story of Gösta Berling." Athenaeum, 8 April 1899, p. 435.

181. Boynton, H. W. "Gösta Berling's Saga." Bookman 49 (April, 1919), 182.

182. "Gösta Berling's Saga." Boston Transcript, 8 January 1919, p. 7.
This reviewer points out the detail Lagerlöf provides of the countryside and the nature of her homeland.

183. "Gösta Berling's Saga." Nation, 8 March 1919, p. 361.

184. "Gösta Berling's Saga." New Republic, 8 March 1919, p. 191.
The reviewer says that Gösta is a truly memorable character. One reason for this is the range and vigor of his emotions.

185. "Gösta Berling's Saga." New York Evening Post, 1 February 1919, p. 2.

186. "Gösta Berling's Saga." Spectator, 10 May 1919, p. 602.

187. "Story of Gösta Berling." Athenaeum, 18 March 1899, p. 335.

188. "Story of Gösta Berling." Bookman 8 (November, 1898), p. 253.

189. "Story of Gösta Berling." Dial, 1 May 1899, p. 310.

190. "Story of Gösta Berling." Fortnightly Review 71 (N. S. 65) (March, 1899), 394-6.

191. "Story of Gösta Berling." Spectator, 28 January 1899, p. 139.

The Treasure

192. Larsen, Hanna Astrup. "The Treasure." New York Tribune, 19 July 1925, p. 5.

193. "The Treasure." Booklist 21 (June, 1925), 340.

194. "The Treasure." Boston Transcript, 27 June 1925, p. 5e.
The reviewer questions the selection of the theme and setting of Lagerlof, but praises her achievement with this selection.

195. "The Treasure." Cleveland Open Shelf, July 1925, p. 81.

196. "The Treasure." Ms 2 (June, 1974), 35.

197. "The Treasure." New York Times Book Review, 19 April 1925, p. 8.
The reviewer sees the virtue of telling the tale set in the sixteenth century in a simple manner, but is not convinced the transition conveys the simplicity intended.

198. "The Treasure." New York World, 1 May 1925, p. 7m.

199. "The Treasure." Pratt Institute Quarterly, Autumn 1925, p. 39.

200. "The Treasure." Saturday Review of Literature, 26 September 1925, p. 164.

The Wonderful Adventures of Nils

201. Birmingham, M. L. "The Wonderful Adventures of Nils." Commonweal, 24 May 1968, p. 304.

202. Cimino, Maria. "The Wonderful Adventures of Nils." New York Times Book Review, 3 March 1968, p. 30.
Cimino states that the new translation, while capturing the clarity and simplicity of the original, "lacks the animation and color of the earlier translation."

203. "The Wonderful Adventures of Nils." Booklist 4 (January, 1908), 22.

204. "The Wonderful Adventures of Nils." Bulletin of the Center for Children's Books 21 (May, 1968), 145.

205. "The Wonderful Adventures of Nils." Independent, 19 December 1907, p. 1479.
This reviewer, as others, praises the book but recognizes the probable limited appeal in America. The reason cited for the limited appeal is a great cultural difference, particularly with modern America.

206. "The Wonderful Adventures of Nils." Kirkus, 1 January 1968, p. 6.

207. "The Wonderful Adventures of Nils." New York Times Saturday Review, 23 November 1907, p. 749.

208. "The Wonderful Adventures of Nils." Publishers' Weekly, 22 January 1968, p. 274.

KNUT HAMSUN
1859-1952

Knut Hamsun's family was from Gudbrandsdalm, a valley in the heart of Norway. His family name was actually Pederson, but Knut took the name of the homestead, a rather common practice in nineteenth-century Norway. He was born of peasant stock. His father was an artisan who worked with metals, but, unfortunately, artisans at this time were not successful financially.

Knut was actually raised by an uncle who was a clergyman. Knut was rather high-strung as a boy and the uncle's method of calming his ward down was frequent beatings and much hard work. The boy's only means of amusement was to go into the cemetery and make up stories about the names he came across.

His uncle arranged an apprenticeship for Knut with a shoemaker soon after he reached the age of confirmation. Knut, however, knew even at that age that his desire was the literary life. He began writing poetry and published a romantic poem entitled "Meeting Again." He soon followed that with a story, "Björger." Naturally, he did not remain with the cobbler long. He spent a short time working on the docks in the town of Bodä. He then set out wandering—a period of his life that lasted ten years. As a means of survival he worked briefly at a number of jobs during this time. Among his jobs were teaching and clerking in a sheriff's office.

That time provided the material for Hamsun's book Wanderers, which includes "Under the Autumn Star" and "A Wanderer Plays with Muted Strings." That work was written long after Hamsun's own period of wandering, written in the light of retrospect. Hamsun attempted to relive some of his lost youth by trying to recreate his wanderings. Looking back after many years Hamsun wrote with a longing for the youth he could not recapture.

In the 1880s many Norwegians emigrated to America in search of economic security. Many authors wrote about that emigration, their heroes usually finding vast new lands and opportunities. Hamsun read books by Björnsen, Ibsen, Kielland, and Lie, and so set out for America himself. Whereas most of the emigrants traveled in search of financial riches, Hamsun went to America in search of opportunities to write. He came away sorely disappointed. He found that America was not paradise for him, so he returned to Norway, where he decided to make his living by writing. One product of his stay in America was a book of observations entitled The Cultural Life of Modern America. The book has a number of inaccuracies and some misinformation, but it does have some shrewd penetrations into the failings of American society.

After his return from America Hamsun spent a few months in Denmark. He approached Eduard Brandes, the editor of the Copenhagen daily, Politiken, with the manuscript for Hunger. Hamsun very closely resembled the hero of his tale, a shabby, tattered, starving figure. Also, as in the story, Brandes mailed a ten-krone note to Hamsun. Brandes compared Hamsun to Dostoevski. The first chapters of Hunger appeared in the magazine New Soil in 1888. The book was published in its entirety in 1890. Publication resulted in immediate notoriety for Hamsun.

With his notoriety came a certain influence for Hamsun. Not only were his first book, Hunger, and his second book, Mysteries, widely read, Hamsun found that his opinions were listened to. He used this opportunity to speak out against the older poets and against standard literary tradition. He used Mysteries and its central figure, Johan Nagel, to express his views. In his lectures Hamsun attacked Ibsen, Tolstoy, and other revered literary personalities. Nagel became Hamsun's voice for criticism.

The 1890s were a very productive decade for Hamsun. In addition to Hunger and Mysteries, he wrote Pan, Shallow Soil, Victoria, and several other books. With Pan, Hamsun first portrayed a major figure's relation to nature. Lieutenant Glahn is a hunter who has lived in the forest for a number of years, so long, in fact, that he has taken on some of the characteristics of the forest animals. In Glahn, Hamsun created a character who is totally comfortable in the woods, in the primitive world. Glahn's world, however, is shattered when he is forced into contact with townspeople. Glahn is awkward and out of place. Through Glahn's experience, Hamsun presented the irreconcilable difference between nature and the city, a theme that he often repeated.

Growth of the Soil, perhaps Hamsun's best-known work, also presents the conflict between nature and the city. It is a book written in praise of those who work the soil. Sivert, the man of the soil, is contrasted with Eleseus, the man of the city. It is clear that Hamsun's sympathies always lie with Sivert. Growth of the Soil was almost a re-creation of the world, at least a discovery of nature. Isak can be likened to Adam in a virgin world.

Growth of the Soil was published in Norway in 1917. It was published in English in 1920, the year Hamsun was awarded the Nobel Prize in literature. By that time he had published a sizeable body of fiction. In fact, the years from 1890 to 1920 were by far the most prolific of his career. After the publication of Women at the Pump in 1920, Hamsun's literary output diminished greatly. At that time, however, he was only just finding an audience for his work.

With the coming of World War II, Hamsun began to harbor pro-Nazi sentiments. He was very outspoken prior to and during the German occupation of Norway. There was little to account for Hamsun's philosophical and ideological beliefs late in his life. Only the results are evident. He was ostracized by his own people and by many other nations, and his countrymen viewed him as a traitor. Little attention was paid to either him or his works from the 1930s until rather recently because of his radical sentiments.

Knut Hamsun died near Grimstad, Norway, on February 19, 1952, at the age of ninety-two. Many of his novels are currently being reprinted and are being critically viewed in the light of the passage of some time. That his was a rare talent cannot be denied now, but it is unfortunate that his political leanings obscured his talent for a generation.

MAJOR WORKS IN ENGLISH

August. Trans. by Eugene Gay-Tifft. New York: Coward-McCann, 1931.

Benoni. Trans. by Arthur G. Chater. New York: Knopf, 1925.

Chapter the Last. Trans. by Arthur G. Chater. New York: Knopf, 1929.

Children of the Age. Trans. by J. S. Scott. New York: Knopf, 1924.

Dreamers. Trans. by W. W. Worster. New York: Knopf, 1921.

Growth of the Soil. Trans. by W. W. Worster, New York: Knopf, 1921.

Hunger. Trans. by George Egerton [pseud.]. New York: Knopf, 1921.
Hunger. Trans. by Robert Bly. New York: Farrar, Straus, & Giroux, 1967.

Look Back on Happiness. Trans. by Paula Wikeng. New York: Coward-McCann, 1940.

Mysteries. Trans. by Arthur G. Chater. New York: Knopf, 1927.
Mysteries. Trans. by Gerry Bothmer. New York: Farrar, Straus, & Giroux, 1971.

Pan. Trans. by W. W. Worster. New York: Knopf, 1921.

The Ring Is Closed. Trans. by Eugene Gay-Tifft. New York: Coward-McCann, 1937.

The Road Leads On. Trans. by Eugene Gay-Tifft. New York: Coward-McCann, 1934.

Rosa. Trans. by Arthur G. Chater. New York: Knopf, 1926.

Segelfoss-town. Trans. by J. S. Scott. New York: Knopf, 1925.

Shallow Soil. Trans. by Carl Christian Hyllested. New York: Scribner's, 1914.

Vagabonds. Trans. by Eugene Gay-Tifft. New York: Coward-McCann, 1930.

Victoria. Trans. by Arthur G. Chater. New York: Knopf, 1923.
Victoria. Trans. by Oliver Stallybrass. New York: Farrar, Straus, & Giroux, 1969.

Wanderers. Trans. by W. W. Worster. New York: Knopf, 1922.
Wanderers. Trans. by Oliver and Gunnvor Stallybrass. New York: Farrar, Straus, & Giroux, 1975.

Women at the Pump. Trans. by Arthur G. Chater. New York: Knopf, 1928.
Women at the Pump. Trans. by Oliver and Gunnvor Stallybrass. New York: Farrar, Straus, & Giroux, 1978.

BOOKS

209. Berendsohn, Walter Arthur. Knut Hamsun. New York: The Revisionist Press, 1971.

210. Larsen, Hanna Astrup. Knut Hamsun. New York: Knopf, 1922.
Larsen's is a somewhat critical biography of Hamsun, but it is more subjective and sentimental than need be. One drawback is that it was written thirty years before Hamsun's death.

211. Skavlan, E. Knut Hamsun. New York: The Revisionist Press, 1971.

DISSERTATIONS

212. Buttry, Dolores Jean. "Knut Hamsun: A Scandinavian Rousseau." Diss. University of Illinois at Urbana-Champaign, 1978.

213. Denton, Frankie Belle. "Hamsun, Strindberg, Rilke: The Limits of the Naturalistic Narrative. A Study of 'Sult,' 'Inferno,' and'Die Aufzeichnungen des Malte Laurids Brigge.'" Diss. University of Texas at Austin, 1977.

214. Ingwersen, Faith Charlene. "The Truthful Liars: A Comparative Analysis of Knut Hamsun's Mysteries and Martin A. Hansen's Loegneren." Diss. University of Chicago, 1974.

215. Kampits, Eva Ida. "Self-Seekers: Vagabonds in the Early Works of Knut Hamsun and Hermann Hesse." Diss. Boston College, 1977.

216. Morgridge, Barbara Gordon. "Knut Hamsun's Literary Relationship to America." Diss. University of Washington, 1975.

217. Nybo, Gregory Peter Ole. "Knut Hamsun's _Mysteries_: A Study in Fictional Technique." Diss. University of California, Berkeley, 1965.

218. Simpson, James Allen, Jr. "Theme and Narrative in Knut Hamsun's _Landstrykere_." Diss. University of California, Berkeley, 1968.

CHAPTERS AND MATERIALS IN BOOKS

219. Allen, W. Gore. "The Nationalists: Knut Hamsun." In _Renaissance in the North_. New York: Sheed & Ward, 1946, pp. 114-28.
The effects of Hamsun's conservatism, even his political conservatism, are viewed in this study. Allen calls for a separation of Hamsun's political extremism and his art.

220. Bach, Giovanni. "Norwegian Literature." In _A History of the Scandinavian Literatures_. Trans. and ed. Frederika Blankner. New York: Dial, 1938, pp. 57-62.

221. Beyer, Harald. "Hamsun and Kinck." In _A History of Norwegian Literature_. New York: New York University Press, 1956, pp. 271-84.
Beyer emphasizes Hamsun's social criticism and his reactionary political leanings, while making a plea (albeit a bit feeble) to separate his art and his politics.

222. Bredsdorff, Elias, Brita Mortensen, and Ronald Popperwell. "Norwegian Literature, 1870-1950." In _An Introduction to Scandinavian Literature from Earliest Times to Our Day_. Cambridge, Eng.: Cambridge University Press, 1951, pp.226-33.

223. Downs, Brian Westerdale. "Kinck and Hamsun." In Modern Norwegian Literature, 1860-1918. Cambridge, Eng.: Cambridge University Press, 1966, pp. 165-88.

Downs takes into account almost all of Hamsun's works in his study. He points out the importance of the wanderer in Hamsun's fiction, along with the vastness of the country, and the mixture of sympathy with ironic detachment.

224. Enright, Dennis Joseph. "Blossoms and Blood: On Knut Hamsun." In Man Is an Onion: Reviews and Essays. La Salle, Ill.: Open Court, 1973, pp. 52-8, rpt. from New York Review of Books, 24 February 1972, p. 42.

225. Ford, Jesse Hill. "Jesse Hill Ford on Knut Hamsun's Growth of the Soil." In Rediscoveries. Ed. David Madden. New York: Crown, 1971, pp. 165-70.

Ford praises Hamsun's imagination and his ability to capture the purpose of life and of mankind.

226. Gustafson, Alrik. "Man and the Soil: Knut Hamsun." In Six Scandinavian Novelists. New York: Princeton University Press, 1940, pp. 226-85.

Like many other critics, Gustafson argues for the consideration of the body of Hamsun's work without regard to his political or social views. He states that Hamsun's best fiction is positive, and depicts the relationship between man and the land.

227. Jorgenson, Theodore. "Neo-Romanticism and Symbolism." In History of Norwegian Literature. New York: Macmillan, 1933, pp. 390-402.

This constitutes a brief sketch of Hamsun and many of his novels. Jorgenson stresses Hamsun's talent as a story-teller.

228. Lavrin, Janko. "Return of Pan (on Knut Hamsun)." In Aspects of Modernism from Wilde to Pirandello. London: Stanley Nott, 1935, pp. 93-111.

Lavrin notes Hamsun's ability and affinity for looking back while recognizing that man cannot go backward in time. Lavrin also notes Hamsun's preoccupation with the soil and with the decadence within man.

229. Lovett, Robert Morse. "Growth of the Soil." In *Preface to Fiction: A Discussion of Great Modern Novels*. Chicago: Thomas S. Rockwell, 1931, pp. 41-52.
Lovett tends to oversimplify and at times underestimate *Growth of the Soil*. He sums it up as "man's struggle with nature."

230. Lowenthal, Leo. "Knut Hamsun." In *Literature and the Image of Man: Sociological Studies of the European Drama and Novel, 1600-1900*. Boston: Beacon Press, 1957, pp. 190-220.
Lowenthal recognizes the recurrent themes in Hamsun's work: nature (which may have been beneficent or brutal), hero-worship (usually "unheroic heroes"), urban society (the middle class), and nihilism (which Lowenthal says is misanthropic in Hamsun).

231. Marble, Annie Russell. "Knut Hamsun and His Novels of Norwegian Life." In *Nobel Prize Winners in Literature, 1901-1931*. New York: Appleton-Century, 1932, pp. 213-23.
In this sketch, Marble notes the omnipresence of the wanderer in Hamsun's novels, and likens some of the traits of his characters to the author himself.

232. Naess, Harald. "Knut Hamsun and Rasmus Anderson." In *Scandinavian Studies*. Ed. Carl F. Bayerschmidt and Erik J. Friis. Seattle: University of Washington Press, 1965, pp. 269-77.
This relates the relationship between Hamsun and a man he met in America, Rasmus B. Anderson, professor of Scandinavian languages at the University of Wisconsin.

233. ______. "Who Was Knut Hamsun's Hero." In *The Hero in Scandinavian Literature*. Ed. John M. Weinstock and Robert T. Rovinsky. Austin, Texas: University of Texas Press, 1975, pp. 63-86.
The hero in Hamsun's fiction, Naess states, is usually outside society. There is a reliance on self-sufficiency in spite of circumstances. Also, Naess notes the power and beauty that is evident through the protagonists.

234. Orbeck, Anders. "Knut Hamsun." In Scandinavian and Slavic Literature. In vol. 10 of The Columbia University Course in Literature. New York: Columbia University Press, 1928, pp. 269-85.

235. Slochower, H. "Imaginative Metaphor." In No Voice Is Wholly Lost. London: Dennis Dobson, Ltd., 1946, pp. 119-21.
Slochower uses selections from Growth of the Soil to depict an attempt to recapture a bit of a simplistic past in the midst of upheaval during World War I.

CRITICAL ARTICLES

236. Berendsohn, Walter Arthur. "Recent Scandinavian Literature." Contemporary Review 154 (July, 1938), 94-6.

237. Bjorkman, Edwin. "Knut Hamsun: From Hunger to Harvest." New Republic, 13 April 1921, pp. 195-7.
Bjorkman speaks of some of the problems of man and of society that Hamsun enters into his novels. He stresses the importance of Hamsun's suggestiveness and of the fact that Hamsun offers no solution.

238. ________. "On Reading Hamsun." Reviewer 2 (October, 1921), 42-3.

239. Bolckmans, Alex. "Henry Miller's Tropic of Cancer and Knut Hamsun's Sult." Scandinavica 14 (November, 1975), 115-26.
Bolckmans notes Hamsun's influence on Henry Miller. He especially notes similarities between Tropic of Cancer and Sult.

240. Cerf, Bennett. "Trade Winds." Saturday Review of Literature, 26 December 1942, p. 15, rpt. in Wilson Library Bulletin 17 (May, 1958), 758.

241. Coles, R. "Knut Hamsun: The Beginning and the End." New Republic, 23 September 1967, pp. 21-4.

242. Eddy, Beverly D. "Hamsun's Victoria and Munch's Livsfrisen: Variations on a Theme." Scandinavian Studies 48 (Spring, 1976), 156-68.

Eddy compares Hamsun and Munch, centering on the parallels of their artistic development. For instance, Hamsun's Victoria and Munch's painting, Livsfrisen, represent major moves away from subjective portrayal to a more epic style and theme.

243. Friederich, Reinhard H. "Kafka and Hamsun's Mysteries." Comparative Literature 28 (Winter, 1976), 34-50.

Friederich discusses Hamsun's Mysteries and the influence of Hamsun on Kafka, particularly in The Trial.

244. Fischer, Heinrich. "The Case of Knut Hamsun." Trans. David Maurice Graham. New Writings and Daylight 6 (1945), 90-100.

Fischer maintains that the Knut Hamsun who embraced Nazism was not the same Knut Hamsun who produced the earlier works. He says that many ideals and ideas died in Hamsun and that the two personalities should not be confused.

245. Flanagan, J. F. "Knut Hamsun's Early Years in the Northwest." Minnesota History 20 (December, 1939), 397-412.

Flanagan discusses Hamsun's visit to America, his disillusionment with America, and the impact of his visit felt by Americans.

246. Haugen, E. "Knut Hamsun and the Nazis." Books Abroad 15 (January, 1941), 17-22.

247. Kauffmann, Stanley. "Stanley Kauffmann on Norway's Forgotten Giant." New Republic, 21 February 1969, pp. 28, 42.

248. Kielland, E. "New Aspects of Norwegian Literature." American-Scandinavian Review 45 (June, 1957), 150.

249. Klienberger, H. R. "The Norwegian Contribution to the Modern Novel: Knut Hamsun and Sigrid Undset." Durham University Journal, n.s. 18 (1957), 70-8.

250. Knapland, Paul. "Knut Hamsun: Triumph and Tragedy." Modern Age 9 (Spring, 1965), 165-74.
Knapland turns his attention to Hamsun's political views and the shadow these views cast on his literary accomplishments, particularly in his homeland.

251. Larsen, Hanna Astrup. "Knut Hamsun." American-Scandinavian Review 9 (July, 1921), 454-5.

252. ________. "New Books in Norway." American-Scandinavian Review 22 (June, 1934), 155.

253. Lesser, J. "Knut Hamsun." Life and Letters Today 22 (August, 1939), 160-6.

254. Lundin, Rolf. "The Scandinavian Reception of Theodore Dreiser." Dreiser Newsletter 6 (September, 1975), 1-8.

255. McFarlane, J. W. "The Whisper of the Blood: A Study of Knut Hamsun's Early Novels." PMLA 71 (September, 1956), 563-94.
McFarlane denies that Hamsun's writing marks a move from the subjective to the objective. Rather, it is a move from a revolt newly-originated against aging fashion to a disregard for the tradition spawned by this revolt.

256. Miller, Henry. "Knut Hamsun and Me." New York Times Book Review, 22 August 1971, pp. 1, 30.

257. Moritzer, J. "Knut Hamsun in Life and Letters." Bookman 52 (January, 1921), 437-41.

258. Muir, Edwin. "Great Writer." The Freeman, 8 August 1923, p. 522.

259. Naess, Harald. "Four Hamsun Letters." Durham University Journal, n.s. 21 (1959), 1-10.

260. _______. "Knut Hamsun and America." Scandinavian Studies 39 (November, 1967), 305-28.

This article concentrates on Hamsun's social philosophy, especially his view of America, American democracy, and American culture in his fiction.

261. _______. "A Strange Meeting and Hamsun's Mysterier." Scandinavian Studies 36 (February, 1964), 48-58.

Naess studies several aspects of Mysterier which he claims are autobiographical. He finds a number of events, places, and characters that correspond to Hamsun's own life.

262. _______. "The Three Hamsuns: The Changing Attitude in Recent Criticism." Scandinavian Studies 32 (August, 1960), 129-39.

Naess treats three periods of the study of Hamsun's literary life: the first Naess marks with Hamsun's receipt of the Nobel Prize, along with over-emphasis on Growth of the Soil; the second is Hamsun's Nazism and the barrage of criticism; and the last has concerned itself with a study of the work separate from the man.

263. Nilson, Sten Sparre. "Knut Hamsun, England, and America." Scandinavica 1 (November, 1962), 124-36.

Nilson examines Hamsun's view of America and England, particularly the social customs and ideas which Hamsun could not abide.

264. "Novels of Knut Hamsun." Littell's Living Age, 4 January 1902, pp. 13-5.

265. Simpson, Allen. "Hamsun and Camus: Consciousness in Markens Grode and 'The Myth of Sisyphus.'" Scandinavian Studies 48 (Summer, 1976), 272-83.

266. Updike, John. "Half-Mad and Maddening." New Yorker, 9 October 1971, p. 169.

Updike states that Mysteries is not as full in its creativity as Hunger, but that it succeeds in making the reader uncomfortable.

267. ________. "Love as a Standoff." New Yorker, 28 June 1969, p. 90.

In reading Victoria, Updike says that Hamsun may have been a bit too romantically contriving. He also states that the novel's success is in the evocation of emotion, rather than in the depiction of characters.

268. ________. "My Mind Was Without a Shadow." New Yorker, 2 December 1967, pp. 223-4.

Updike states that Hamsun is not outdated, but that Hunger and On Overgrown Paths can still be read with freshness. The above three articles have been reprinted in Updike's collection of essays, Picked-Up Pieces. New York: Knopf, 1975, pp. 141-53.

269. ________. "A Primal Modern." New Yorker, 23 May 1976, pp. 116-8.

Updike's focus is on The Wanderer and he speaks of the desolation that the wanderer finds and that drove him to wander in the first place.

270. ________. "Saddled with the World." New Yorker, 23 October 1978, pp. 176-82.

Updike concentrates on The Women at the Pump in this article. He recognizes the geographical and temporal distance between the American reader and Hamsun.

271. Van Marken, Amy. "One of Knut Hamsun's Female Main Characters, Julie d'Espard." Scandinavica 13 (November, 1974), 107-15.

In her study of one character, van Marken notes the themes present in most of Hamsun's works, most notably the decay of the city and the nobility of nature and the woman's place in the world Hamsun creates.

272. Wiehr, Josef. "Knut Hamsun, His Personality and His Outlook on Life." Smith College Studies in Modern Languages 3 (October, 1921-January, 1922), 1-129.

Wiehr's study, which comprises the entire issue of Smith College Studies in Modern Languages, views the body of Hamsun's work (to the date of Wiehr's writing) in the context of the author's own beliefs and personal philosophy, inasmuch as it can be said that Hamsun had a strictly formulated and consistent personal philosophy. The study stresses Hamsun's optimism rather than the pessimism that is also evident throughout his novels. In so doing, Wiehr's study does not do justice to Hamsun's rather revolutionary early works, which deal with the displacement of man and in which optimism is apparent only when Hamsun turns his attention to nature.

273. Worster, W. H. "Writings of Knut Hamsun." Fortune 114 (December, 1920), 1003-13.

BOOK REVIEWS

August

274. "August." Booklist 28 (December, 1931), 151.

275. "August." Cleveland Open Shelf, December 1931, p. 146.

276. "August." Pittsburgh Monthly Bulletin 37 (January, 1932), 4.

277. "August." Springfield Republican, 15 November 1931, p. 7e.

278. Hutchison, Percy. "August." New York Times Book Review, 25 October 1931, p. 7.
Hutchison views August as a sign of the maturation of Hamsun, both as a writer and as a person.

279. Olson, A. L. "August." New York Times Book Review, 4 January 1932, p. 8.

280. Roberts, Brian. "August." Life and Letters 8 (1932), 478.

281. Rolvaag, O. E. "August." New York Herald-Tribune Books, 25 October 1931, p. 5.
Rolvaag claims that August and Vagabonds are both superior to and will outlive Hamsun's more successful and more popular Growth of the Soil.

282. Young, D. M. "August." New Republic, 16 December 1931, p. 142.
Young is of the opinion that August is not a particularly memorable character, and that the translation of the 1931 edition is flawed.

Benoni

283. "Benoni." Booklist 22 (December, 1925), 117.

284. "Benoni." Boston Transcript, 14 October 1925, p. 4.

285. "Benoni." New York Times Book Review, 30 August 1925, p. 8.

286. "Benoni." Springfield Republican, 29 November 1925, p. 7a.
The reviewer praises Hamsun for creating a vision of Norway that readers all over the world can appreciate.

287. Gjelsner, R. H. "Benoni." New York Tribune, 18 October 1925, p. 11.

288. Larsen, Hanna Astrup. "Benoni." Literary Digest International Book Review, October 1925, p. 740.

289. Paterson, Isabel. "Benoni." Bookman 62 (September, 1925), 86.
Paterson states that the story and the telling of Benoni are simple and the novel is uninteresting because of this simplicity.

Chapter the Last

290. "Chapter the Last." Boston Transcript, 11 October 1929, p. 3.

291. Codman, Florence. "Chapter the Last." Nation, 23 October 1929, p. 468.

292. Coxe, Howard. "Chapter the Last." New Republic, 25 December 1929, p. 149.

293. Dawson, M. C. "Chapter the Last." New York Herald-Tribune Books, 22 September 1929, p. 3.

294. Fadiman, C. P. "Chapter the Last." Bookman 70 (November, 1929), 312.
Fadiman says that Chapter the Last is not as tightly structured as some of Hamsun's other novels, but he thinks it is still superior to most contemporary American writing.

295. Hutchison, Percy. "Chapter the Last." New York Times Book Review, 22 September 1929, p. 9.
Hutchison notes the excellence of Hamsun's writing and also finds the novel to hopeful and uplifting.

Children of the Age

296. Allen, R. H. "Children of the Age." Boston Transcript, 16 February 1924, p. 5.
Allen praises Hamsun's directness in telling a story, and the constancy of motion in this novel.

297. Anderson, I. "Children of the Age." Literary Digest International Book Review, April 1924, p. 394.

298. "Children of the Age." Booklist 20 (May, 1924), 300.

299. "Children of the Age." Nation and Athenaeum, 24 May 1924, sup. 258.

300. "Children of the Age." New Republic, 2 July 1924, p. 166.

301. "Children of the Age." New York Times Book Review, 3 February 1924, p. 8.

302. "Children of the Age." The Times (London) Literary Supplement, 13 November 1924, p. 728.

303. Hartley, L. P. "Children of the Age." Spectator, 31 May 1924, p. 885.

304. Krutch, J. W. "Children of the Age." Nation, 14 May 1924, p. 563.

305. Porterfield, A. W. "Children of the Age." Bookman 59 (April, 1924), 233.

306. ________. "Children of the Age." Literary Review of the New York Evening Post, 31 May 1924, p. 787.
In this review Porterfield notes that Children of the Age is, in many ways, a reiteration of previously stated Hamsun themes.

307. Stagg, Hunter. "Children of the Age." Reviewer 4 (April, 1924), 240-1.

308. Wright, Ralph. "Children of the Age." New Statesman, 24 May 1924, p. 196.

Dreamers

309. "Dreamers." Bookman 54 (January, 1922), 493.

310. "Dreamers." Boston Transcript, 7 December 1921, p. 9.
The reviewer states that Hamsun's genius lies not in his psychological investigation, but in his human insight.

311. "Dreamers." New York Times Book Review, 8 January 1922, p. 10.

Growth of the Soil

312. Baerlein, Henry. "Growth of the Soil." Bookman (London) 59 (December, 1920), 140-1.

313. Boyd, Ernest. "Growth of the Soil." Literary Review of the New York Evening Post, 5 March 1921, p. 3.
Boyd calls the novel "poignant" and says that it is superior to Hamsun's earlier novels, Hunger and Pan.

314. Boynton, H. W. "Growth of the Soil." Weekly Review, 6 April 1921, p. 320.
Boynton says that Growth of the Soil is consistent and faithful in its realism and that it is deserving of the term "Epic."

315. Goldberg, I. "Growth of the Soil." Boston Transcript, 19 March 1921, p. 8.
Goldberg says that he has difficulty finding words to express his praise for this novel.

316. "Growth of the Soil." Athenaeum, 11 June 1920, p. 767.

317. "Growth of the Soil." Best Sellers, 1 July 1972, p. 179.

318. "Growth of the Soil." Booklist 17 (March, 1921), 218.

319. "Growth of the Soil." Bookman 53 (June, 1921), 351.

320. "Growth of the Soil." Cleveland Open Shelf, April 1921, p. 26.

321. "Growth of the Soil." Dial 71 (August, 1921), 242.

322. "Growth of the Soil." Grennell Review 16 (June, 1921), 450.

323. "Growth of the Soil." Independent and Weekly Review, 17 September 1921, p. 133.

324. "Growth of the Soil." Nation, 30 March 1921, p. 486.

325. "Growth of the Soil." New York Times Book Review, 13 March 1921, p. 15.

326. "Growth of the Soil." Reviewer, 1 April 1921, pp. 120-1.

327. "Growth of the Soil." The Times (London) Literary Supplement, 6 May 1921, p. 285.

328. "Growth of the Soil." Wisconsin Library Bulletin 17 (October, 1921), 156.

329. Gustafson, Alrik. "Hamsun's Growth of the Soil." American-Scandinavian Review 27 (September, 1939), 198-214.

330. Holcomb, G. "Growth of the Soil." American Art Journal 10 (1978), 33.

331. Proctor, Dub. "Growth of the Soil." Publishers Weekly, 19 February 1921, p. 576.

332. Stagg, Hunter. "Growth of the Soil." Reviewer, 4 (April, 1924), 336-7.

Hunger

333. Coles, Robert. "*Hunger*." *New Republic*, 23 September 1967, p. 21.

334. Doyle, P. A. "*Hunger*." *Best Sellers*, 1 August 1967, p. 169.

335. Eliot, R. F. "*Hunger*." *Publishers Weekly*, 18 December, 1920, p. 1884.
Eliot sees hints of humor in *Hunger* that relieve the tension and depression, though there is actually no relief to be found.

336. Fallowell, Duncan. "*Hunger*." *Books and Bookmen* 20 (August, 1975), 59.

337. "*Hunger*." *Book World*, 13 April 1975, p. 4.

338. "*Hunger*." *Bookman* (London) 60 (April, 1921), 72.

339. "*Hunger*." *Dial* 70 (January, 1921), 106.
The reviewer notes that *Hunger* is obviously a product of the naturalism of the last century, but that it finds an audience in America in this century.

340. "*Hunger*." *Kirkus*, 15 May 1967, p. 618.

341. "*Hunger*." *Listener*, 28 February 1974, p. 281.

342. "*Hunger*." *Nation*, 26 January 1921, p. 122.

343. "*Hunger*." *New York Times Book Review*, 12 December 1920, p. 20.
This reviewer recognizes the quality of *Hunger*, but states that some readers may find it distressing or even apalling.

344. "*Hunger*." *Observer*, 3 March 1974, p. 36.

345. "*Hunger*." *Reviewer*, 15 February 1921, pp. 23-4.

346. "*Hunger*." *Springfield Republican*, 7 December 1920, p. 8.

347. "Hunger." The Times (London) Literary Supplement, 6 May 1921, p. 285.

348. Level, Edith. "Hunger." Library Journal 92 (July, 1967), 2605.

349. Maloff, Saul. "Hunger." Newsweek, 31 July 1967, p. 75.

350. Schott, W. "Hunger." Life, 1 September 1967, p. 6.

351. Williams, Hugo. "Demons." New Statesman, 29 March 1974, p. 455.

Look Back on Happiness

352. Clark, M. E. "Look Back on Happiness." Library Journal, 1 April 1940, p. 300.

353. Fadiman, C. P. "Look Back on Happiness." New Yorker, 13 April 1940, p. 96.
In reviewing Look Back on Happiness Fadiman sees the level of of eccentricity which Hamsun has reached and the effects of this on his writing.

354. Fainsad, E. S. "Look Back on Happiness." Boston Transcript, 4 May 1940, p. 2.

355. Geismar, Maxwell. "Look Back on Happiness." New York Herald-Tribune Books, 7 April 1940, p. 6.
Geismar sees this novel as being closer to Hamsun's own belief than any other. He notes Hamsun's misanthropy struggling against his wish to save mankind.

356. Larrson, Gosta. "Look Back on Happiness." Saturday Review of Literature, 6 April 1940, p. 18.

357. Littell, Robert. "Look Back on Happiness." Yale Review 29 (Summer, 1940), xiii.

358. "Look Back on Happiness." Nation, 18 May 1940, p. 634.

359. "Look Back on Happiness." New Republic, 20 May 1940, p. 682.

360. "Look Back on Happiness." New York Times Book Review, 7 April 1940, p. 2.

361. "Look Back on Happiness." Time, 15 April 1940, p. 100.

362. Skillen, Edward, Jr. "Look Back on Happiness." Commonweal, 19 April 1940, p. 556.

Mysteries

363. Blyth, R. "Mysteries." Listener, 10 January 1974, p. 56.

364. De Feo, Ronald. "Mysteries." Nation, 28 February 1972, p. 278.

365. Greacen, Robert. "Mysteries." Books and Bookmen 19 (May, 1974), 86.

366. Hutchison, Percy. "Mysteries." New York Times Book Review, 1 May 1927, p. 7.
Hutchison recognizes Hamsun's ability to depict passion and the baser qualities of man.

367. Knight, Susan. "Northern Lights." New Statesman, 30 November 1973, pp. 827-8.

368. Lehmann-Haupt, C. "Mysteries." New York Times Book Review, 25 August 1971, p. 35.

369. "Mysteries." Antioch Review 31 (Fall, 1971), 438.

370. "Mysteries." Booklist 24 (October, 1927), 27.

371. "Mysteries." Booklist, 1 October 1971, p. 131.

372. "Mysteries." Boston Transcript, 11 June 1927, p. 5.

373. "Mysteries." Choice 8 (February, 1972), 1588.

374. "Mysteries." Cleveland Open Shelf, July 1927, p. 88.

375. "Mysteries." Kirkus, 15 May 1971, p. 576.

376. "Mysteries." Nation and Athenaeum, 11 June 1927, p. 342.

377. "Mysteries." National Observer, 30 August 1971, p. 17.

378. "Mysteries." New Orleans Times-Picayune, 24 February 1972, sec. 5, p. 10.

379. "Mysteries." New Statesman." 21 May 1927, p. 186.

380. "Mysteries." New York Times Book Review, 5 December 1971, p. 84.

381. "Mysteries." Newsweek, 27 December 1971, p. 61.

382. "Mysteries." Spectator, 28 May 1927, p. 957.

383. "Mysteries." The Times (London) Literary Supplement, 16 August 1927, p. 560.

The reviewer's primary criticism of the book is that it seems to be almost totally without logic. Despite this, the reviewer says there are clear characterizations.

384. O'Hara, J. D. "Mysteries." Book World, 16 January 1972, p. 10.

385. Porterfield, A. W. "The Hamsun Follies of 1892." Saturday Review of Literature, 11 June 1927, p. 896.

386. Prescott, P. S. "Mysteries." Newsweek, 6 September 1971, p. 68.

387. Rosenthal, Raymond. "Mysteries." Saturday Review, 28 August 1971, p. 26.

388. Spector, Robert Donald. "Mysteries." Scandinavian Studies 45 (Winter, 1973), 79.

389. Steen, Signe L. "Mysteries." Library Journal 96 (July, 1971), 2346.

390. Walpole, Hugh. "Mysteries." New York Herald-Tribune Books, 22 May 1927, p. 1.

Pan

391. Boynton, H. W. "Pan." Weekly Review, 27 August 1921, p. 193.

392. Field, L. M. "Pan." New York Times Book Review, 31 July 1921, p. 24.
Field is of the opinion that Pan is particularly excellent in its quality and in its evocation of pathos.

393. Goldberg, I. "Pan." Boston Transcript, 6 August 1921, p. 4.

394. Lovett, R. M. "Pan." New Republic, 31 August 1921, p. 25.

395. "Pan." Athenaeum, 24 December 1920, p. 866.
This reviewer states that Pan is fragmentary in comparison to some of Hamsun's other works.

396. "Pan." Nation, 14 September 1921, p. 198.

397. "Pan." Springfield Republican, 28 August 1921, p. 9a.

398. Stagg, Hunter. "Pan." Reviewer 2 (October, 1921), 55.

Prairie

399. "Prairie." Littell's Living Age, 27 August 1921, pp. 549-50.

The Ring Is Closed

400. Carleton, P. D. "The Ring Is Closed." Saturday Review of Literature, 29 May 1937, p. 7.

401. Hutchison, Percy. "The Ring Is Closed." New York Times Book Review, 9 May 1937, p. 5.

402. Mann, D. L. "The Ring Is Closed." Boston Transcript, 19 June 1937, p. 2.

403. Mitchneck, S. A. "The Ring Is Closed." New York Herald-Tribune Books, 9 May 1937, p. 4.

404. "The Ring Is Closed." Booklist, 33 (July, 1937), 339.

405. "The Ring Is Closed." Christian Science Monitor, 28 May 1937, p. 18.

406. "The Ring Is Closed." Pratt Institute Quarterly, Autumn 1937, p. 33.

407. "The Ring Is Closed." Wisconsin Library Bulletin 33 (July, 1937), 131.

408. Sayers, Michael. "The Ring Is Closed." New Republic, 4 August 1937, p. 371.

Sayers states that although Hamsun is a master craftsman, this novel seems to be pointless. He is particularly discouraged by the portrayal of Abel, the book's main character.

409. Young, Stanley. "The Ring Is Closed." Nation, 15 May 1937, p. 568.

Young sees similarities of vision between this novel and Hunger, although the two works were written nearly fifty years apart.

The Road Leads On

410. Brickell, Herschel. "The Road Leads On." North American Review 238 (August, 1934), 187.

411. Butcher, Fanny. "The Road Leads On." Chicago Daily Tribune, 16 June 1934, p. 10.

412. Frank, Grace. "The Road Leads On." Saturday Review of Literature, 16 June 1934, p. 753.
Frank recommends The Road Leads On, but finds fault with the translation of the 1934 edition.

413. Hutchison, Percy. "The Road Leads On." New York Times Book Review, 17 June 1934, p. 1.

414. Matthews, T. S. "The Road Leads On." New Republic, 18 July 1934, p. 271.

415. "The Road Leads On." Booklist 30 (July, 1934), 351.

416. "The Road Leads On." Boston Transcript, 9 June 1934, p. 1.

417. "The Road Leads On." Cleveland Open Shelf, May 1934, p. 12.

418. "The Road Leads On." Nation, 20 June 1934, p. 712.

419. "The Road Leads On." Pratt Institute Quarterly, Autumn 1934, p. 38.

420. "The Road Leads On." Springfield Republican, 24 June 1934, p. 7e.

421. "The Road Leads On." Wisconsin Library Bulletin 30 (October, 1934), 187.

422. Ross, Mary. "The Road Leads On." New York Herald-Tribune Books, 17 June 1934, p. 1.
Ross chooses to view the novel as a celebration of mankind and of the simple life.

423. Thompson, Frederick. "The Road Leads On." Commonweal, 20 July 1934, p. 313.

Rosa

424. Bjorkman, Edwin. "Rosa." New York Herald-Tribune Books, 11 April 1926, p. 18.

425. Crawford, J. W. "Rosa." Literary Digest International Book Review, April 1926, p. 326.
Crawford was impressed by the lyrical quality of Hamsun's prose and notes that Rosa broaches no controversial issues, but is engaging.

426. "Rosa." Booklist 22 (May, 1926), 330.

427. "Rosa." Boston Transcript, 24 February 1926, p. 4.

428. "Rosa." Cleveland Open Shelf, April 1926, p. 53.

429. "Rosa." Living Age, 19 June 1926, p. 648.

430. "Rosa." New York Times Book Review, 7 February 1926, p. 8.
The reviewer notes the absence of somber mood and depression, but he finds the humor of the novel a bit ponderous. He makes a number of generalizations, some unfounded, about Scandinavian literature and its melancholia and attempts at humor.

431. Short, L. S. "Rosa." Literary Review of the New York Evening Post, 27 February 1926, p. 7.

Segelfoss-town

432. Bjorkman, Edwin. "Segelfoss-town." Literary Digest International Book Review, April 1925, p. 354.
Bjorkman recognizes the black humor and occasional bitterness of the novel, likening it to Dickens.

433. ________. "Segelfoss-town." Literary Review of the New York Evening Post, 9 May 1925, p. 4.
Bjorkman states in this review that Segelfoss-town is "amusing," "touching," and "alluring."

434. Boyd, Ernest. "Segelfoss-town." Bookman 61 (May, 1925), 354.

435. Hodgin, D. G. "Segelfoss-town." Reviewer 5 (October, 1925), 117-8.

436. Kennedy, P. C. "Segelfoss-town." New Statesman, 18 July 1925, p. 397.

437. Muir, Edwin. "Segelfoss-town." Nation and Athenaeum, 20 June 1925, p. 372.

438. Porterfield, A. W. "Segelfoss-town." Bookman 61 (April, 1925), 244.

439. ________. "Segelfoss-town." Saturday Review of Literature, 30 May 1925, p. 787.

440. Richt, Adrian. "Segelfoss-town." New York World, 15 February 1925, p. 7m.
Richt is of the opinion that Segelfoss-town is "either too long or too unresolved in form."

441. "Segelfoss-town." Booklist 21 (May, 1925), 302.

442. "Segelfoss-town." Boston Transcript, 21 March 1925, p. 2.

443. "Segelfoss-town." Cleveland Open Shelf, July 1925, p. 81.

444. "Segelfoss-town." Dial 79 (September, 1925), 259.

445. "Segelfoss-town." New York Times Book Review, 15 February 1925, p. 8.

446. "Segelfoss-town." Pratt Institute Quarterly, Autumn 1925, p. 39.

447. "Segelfoss-town." Springfield Republican, 1 March 1925, p. 7a.

448. "Segelfoss-town." The Times (London) Literary Supplement, 9 July 1925, p. 8.

449. "Segelfoss-town." Wisconsin Library Bulletin 21 (March, 1925), 91.

450. Wolf, R. L. "Segelfoss-town." New York Tribune, 8 March 1925, p. 3

Shallow Soil

451. Boynton, H. W. "Shallow Soil." Nation, 2 April 1914, p. 363.

452. Cary. Lucian. "Shallow Soil." Dial, 1 July 1914, p. 20.

453. Cooper, T. "Shallow Soil." Bookman, 14 May 1914, p. 326.

Cooper states that the novel is uneven, but the reader can catch glimmers of greatness in it.

454. Mann, D. L. "Shallow Soil." Boston Transcript, 1 April 1914, p. 24.

455. "Shallow Soil." Athenaeum, 23 May 1914 (sup.), p. 740.

456. "Shallow Soil." New York Times Book Review, 22 March 1914, p. 136.
The reviewer finds Shallow Soil to be a well-constructed, uniformly interesting work. He also states that the translation of the 1914 edition is quite good.

457. "Shallow Soil." Outlook, 16 May 1914, p. 134.

458. "Shallow Soil." Review of Reviews, 14 May 1914, p. 625.

459. "Shallow Soil." Spectator, 15 August 1914, p. 240.

460. "Shallow Soil." Springfield Republican, 3 September 1914, p. 5.

Vagabonds

461. Calverton, V. F. "Vagabonds." Nation, 12 November 1930, p. 528.
Calverton, perhaps in a moment of patriotic fervor, says that no major American novelist has ever written a book as dull as Vagabonds. He states that Hamsun never lived up to the potential displayed in his early work; he merely grew old.

462. Carleton, Philip D. "Vagabonds." Saturday Review of Literature, 8 November 1930, p. 305.

463. Gay-Tifft, Eugene. "Vagabonds." Life and Letters 7 (1931), 149-51.

464. Hutchison, Percy. "Vagabonds." New York Times Book Review, 2 November 1930, p. 7.
In contrast to Calverton, Hutchison finds Vagabonds compelling. He states that it is "one of the finest and most truly profound of [Hamsun's] works."

465. Kronenberger, Louis. "*Vagabonds*." *New York Herald-Tribune Books*, 2 November 1930, p. 3.
Kronenberger says that *Growth of the Soil* is epic, but the rest of Hamsun's works are ethnic. In his opinion, Norway is the main character of the novels.

466. Robbins, F. L. "*Vagabonds*." *Outlook*, 5 November 1930, p. 387.

467. Salpeter, Harry. "*Vagabonds*." *New York World*, 5 November 1930, p. 3e.

468. "*Vagabonds*." *Booklist* 27 (January, 1931), 208.

469. "*Vagabonds*." *Bookman* 72 (November, 1930), viii.

470. "*Vagabonds*." *Cleveland Open Shelf*, December 1930, p. 147.

471. "*Vagabonds*." *Pittsburgh Monthly Bulletin* 35 (December, 1930), 88.

472. "*Vagabonds*." *Springfield Republican*, 28 December 1930, p. 7e.

Victoria

473. Davenport, Guy. "*Victoria*." *National Review*, 25 March 1969, p. 289.

474. Fjelde, Rolf. "*Victoria*." *New York Times Book Review*, 20 July 1969, p. 30.

475. Gould, Gerald. "*Victoria*." *Saturday Review of Literature*, 12 May 1923, p. 638.

476. Hill, W. B. "*Victoria*." *Best Sellers*, 15 February 1966, p. 464.

477. Leighton, Edith. "*Victoria*." *New York Tribune*, 14 October 1923, p. 27.

478. Loving, Pierre. "*Victoria*." *Nation*, 6 June 1923, p. 663.
Loving says that Hamsun captures the range of emotion in the novel and even captures Victoria's memory and spirit.

479. MacLean, A. "*Victoria*." *The Times (London) Literary Supplement*, 8 November 1974, p. 1249.

480. Moritzer, Julia. "*Victoria*." *Literary Digest International Book Review*, August 1923, p. 30.

481. Morse, J. Mitchell. "*Victoria*." *Hudson Review* 22 (Summer, 1969), 326-7.

482. Muir, Edwin. "*Victoria*." *Freeman*, 8 August 1923, p. 522.

483. Thompson, Lawrence S. "*Victoria*." *Library Journal*, 15 February 1969, p. 779.

484. "*Victoria*." *Booklist* 19 (July, 1923), 318.

485. "*Victoria*." *Choice* 7 (June, 1970), 552.

486. "*Victoria*." *Cleveland Open Shelf*, May 1923, p. 39.

487. "*Victoria*." *New Republic*, 1 August 1923, p. 266.
The reviewer recognizes the necessity of reading *Victoria* as a study of Hamsun's literary progression, but says that the novel is not noteworthy in itself.

488. "*Victoria*." *New York Times Book Review*, 6 May 1923, p. 11.

489. "*Victoria*." *Publishers Weekly*, 4 August 1923, p. 50.

490. "*Victoria*." *Saturday Review*, 27 December 1969, pp. 32-3.

491. "*Victoria*." *Spectator*, 4 August 1923, p. 162.

492. "*Victoria*." *The Times (London) Literary Supplement*, 17 May 1923, p. 341.
The reviewer states that the novel was outdated in its ideas by 1923 and that it is not in keeping with the body of Hamsun's work.

493. "Victoria." Wisconsin Library Bulletin 19 (July, 1923), 413.

Wanderers

494. Allen, Bruce. "Wanderers." Library Journal, 1 September 1975, p. 1570.

495. Cahill, E. H. "Wanderers." Literary Review of the New York Evening Post, 15 July 1922, p. 803.

496. Goldberg, I. "Wanderers." Boston Transcript, 22 March 1922, p. 4.

497. Hawthorne, Hildegarde. "Wanderers." New York Times Book Review, 9 July 1922, p. 5.

498. Keller, Hans. "Wanderers." Freeman, 27 December 1922, p. 382.

499. ________. "Wanderers." The Times (London) Literary Supplement, 21 May 1976, p. 618.

500. Kennedy, Eileen. "Wanderers." Best Sellers 35 (August, 1975), 121.

501. Krutch, J. W. "Wanderers." Nation, 10 May 1922, p. 572.

502. O'Hara, J. D. "Wanderers." New York Times Book Review, 27 July 1975, p. 6.

503. Reid, Forrest. "Wanderers." Nation and Athenaeum, 30 September 1922, p. 858.

Reid recognizes that Wanderers is flawed, but is laudatory of the sustained fluid quality of the novel.

504. Rickert, Edith. "Wanderers." New Republic, 13 September 1922, p. 78.

505. "Wanderers." Bookman (London) 61 (March, 1922), 270.

506. "Wanderers." Choice 13 (March, 1976), 75.

507. "Wanderers." Cleveland Open Shelf, April 1922, p. 27.

508. "Wanderers." Kirkus, 15 April 1975, p. 476.

509. "Wanderers." New Orleans Times Picayune, 14 August 1975, sec. 4, p. 7.

510. "Wanderers." Pittsburgh Monthly Bulletin 27 (June, 1922), 261.

511. "Wanderers." Pratt Institute Quarterly, Autumn 1922, p. 35.

512. "Wanderers." Publishers Weekly, 28 April 1975, p. 40.

513. "Wanderers." Saturday Review of Literature, 4 February 1922, p. 122.

514. "Wanderers." Springfield Republican, 26 April 1922, p. 12.

515. "Wanderers." The Times (London) Literary Supplement, 26 January 1922, p. 59.

The reviewer states that the narrative of Wanderers is incoherent, and that the fault may lie either with Hamsun or with the translator of the 1922 edition.

516. "Wanderers." The Times (London) Literary Supplement, 5 December 1975, p. 1439.

517. West, Rebecca. "Wanderers." New Republic, 5 August 1922, p. 489.

West states that Hamsun's strongest asset is his knowledge of the development of the people of whom he writes.

The Women at the Pump

518. Connolly, Cyril. "The Women at the Pump." New Statesman, 1 December 1928, p. 258.

519. Hartley, L. P. "The Women at the Pump." Saturday Review of Literature, 3 November 1928, p. 582.

520. Lawson, S. "The Women at the Pump." Chicago Review 30 (Spring, 1979), 102-7.

521. Lohrke, Eugene. "The Women at the Pump." New York Herald-Tribune Books, 9 December 1928, p. 31.

522. Messerli, D. "The Women at the Pump." Book World, 27 August 1978, p. 4.

523. Slesinger, Ters. "The Women at the Pump." New York Evening Post, 3 November 1928, p. 8m.

524. Soete, George J. "The Women at the Pump." Library Journal 103 (August, 1978), 1530-1.

525. "The Women at the Pump." Best Sellers 38 (December, 1978), 267.

526. "The Women at the Pump." Book World, 22 July 1979, p. C2.

527. "The Women at the Pump." Boston Transcript, 20 October 1928, p. 6.

528. "The Women at the Pump." Choice 15 (February, 1979), 1670.

529. "The Women at the Pump." Contemporary Review 234 (January, 1979), 48.

530. "The Women at the Pump." Listener, 21 December 1978, p. 864.

531. "The Women at the Pump." Nation, 5 December 1928, p. 639.

The reviewer stresses the quality of Hamsun's humor, which, he admits, is seldom evident in Hamsun's novels.

532. "The Women at the Pump." Nation and Athenaeum, 24 November 1928, p. 300.

This reviewer says that The Women at the Pump is "almost intolerably dull," and he finds it infuriating to read.

533. "The Women at the Pump." New Republic, 7 November 1928, p. 335.

534. "The Women at the Pump." New York Times Book Review, 21 October 1928, p. 5.

535. "The Women at the Pump." New York Times Book Review, 29 July 1979, p. 27.

536. "The Women at the Pump." Publishers Weekly, 15 May 1978, p. 92.

537. "The Women at the Pump." Punch, 13 December 1978, p. 1071.

538. "The Women at the Pump." Saturday Review of Literature, 29 December 1928, p. 564.

539. "The Women at the Pump." The Times (London) Literary Supplement, 25 October 1928, p. 778.

SIGRID UNDSET
1882-1949

Sigrid Undset, the eldest daughter of Ingvald and Anna Charlotte Undset, was born on May 20, 1882, in the Danish town of Kalundborg. When she was two years old the family moved to Christiania. The Undsets would make summer trips back to Kalundborg, though, and, like Selma Lagerlöf, Sigrid Undset would listen attentively to the stories her aunt told her during those visits. The tales were so vividly told that Sigrid sometimes viewed them as part of her own experience.

Sigrid's father had a position with the archeology section of the University Museum in Christiania. His health was poor, though, and, after several moves, it became necessary for the family to live in a rather gloomy section of Christiania, near the Museum. He died in 1893 and, because of financial problems, the family moved to poorer but brighter quarters. Sigrid Undset insisted her childhood was happy, however. She loved and respected her mother and enjoyed her summers spent in Kalundborg.

Sigrid's early education was of a decidedly liberal (politically) nature. Her parents enrolled her at a private coeducational school run by Frau Ragna Nielsen. She had already learned much from her father and found little to interest her in textbooks. Her mother strongly objected to sentimental literature, but Sigrid managed to read some cheap romances on the sly. These were not wholly to her liking though, and neither were the German stories she read in school. She found Hans Christian Andersen much more suited to her taste than Louisa May Alcott. Folktales exerted a strong influence on her youth and on her writing.

The religious upbringing of Sigrid Undset was a bit confused. She was raised in an outwardly conventional manner, but her parents were religiously skeptical. Her father and mother had their notions of God that did not agree with the teaching Sigrid received in school. She was confirmed by an orthodox Lutheran minister who had yet another concept of God. The multitude of opinions left the young Sigrid with nothing firm or substantial to believe in.

In an effort to become self-supporting Sigrid went to a commercial school and took a secretarial position with the electric company. She stayed at that job from 1899 to 1909. The most positive aspect of the job was that she was exposed to different types of people. It gave her a greater appreciation of the city, also.

While she worked in the office she used her spare time to read as widely as she could. She read Shakespeare,

Dickens, Fielding, Shelley, and others. She also read the works of most Norwegian writers. During this time her attention was drawn to the Middle Ages. She was especially interested in medieval sagas and legends. Her extensive study of the Middle Ages provided the foundation for much of her writing. Her first novel, however, had a modern setting, due primarily to the advice of Peter Nansen, director of the Gyldendal publishing house. So, she wrote Fra Marta Oulie, a novel in diary form that deals with infidelity in marriage.

She soon discarded Nansen's advice and wrote Gunnar's Daughter, set in tenth-century Norway and Iceland. It had been influenced in part by her reading of Njal's Saga. In Gunnar's Daughter Sigrid added a modern texture to the description and style of the novel. It is not totally characteristic of the saga.

After the publication of Gunnar's Daughter Sigrid gave up her secretarial job. She received a government travel grant and went to Rome in the summer of 1910. While there she met the artist Anders Svarstad, whom she later married. She corresponded with the Oslo newspaper, Aftenposten, describing Rome and the Campagna. She also described many of the churches and some of the Catholic services, but the spirituality of the occasion left her unimpressed.

In 1911 she published Jenny, the most successful of her novels until then, and the first to be published in English.

It was a controversial novel, though. Many workers for women's rights denounced it as being counterproductive to their cause. Female literary figures were divided in their opinions of the novel. Many readers were opposed to the sexual frankness of some passages and the clinical details of pregnancy and childbirth. Despite the controversy the novel made something of name for Sigrid Undset.

In 1919 Sigrid and her husband moved to Lillehammer in the Gudbrandsdal valley. There she once again took up her study of history, and began to work on her trilogy, Kristin Lavransdatter. The Bridal Wreath was published in 1920, The Mistress of Husaby in 1921, and The Cross in 1922. Her studies of the Middle Ages did not represent a retreat into a world of romanticism. Though she was disillusioned with some aspects of the modern world, she studied the Middle Ages with an objective viewpoint.

In her studies she examined the spread of Christianity throughout Scandinavia. Her investigations led her to Catholicism, where she discovered the meshing of some of her ideas with Church doctrine. She felt it allowed her personal growth without a puritanical kind of morality. Her own conversion provided inspiration for two novels, The Wild Orchid and The Burning Bush, both of which deal with conversion to Catholicism.

Sigrid Undset's writings on Catholicism, in particular her references to the Nazi persecution of Jews, prompted a reaction from Nazi Germany. Many Germans claimed that she was a destructive enemy of Nazism, one to rival the Catholic Church itself. When war broke out and Germany invaded her native Norway she found herself forced into exile. She made her way to America via Russia and Japan. While in America she wrote vehemently against Nazism and Germany.

After the war she returned to Lillehammer, where she died on June 10, 1949. During her lifetime she received most of the honors a writer could earn. In 1928 she was awarded the Nobel Prize in literature. On her birthday in 1947 she received the Grand Cross of the Order of Saint Olav from King Haakon VII. She never stopped working, though, and at the time of her death she was partially finished writing an article on Edmund Burke.

MAJOR WORKS IN ENGLISH

The Axe. Trans. by Arthur G. Chater. New York: Grosset & Dunlap, 1928.

The Bridal Wreath. Trans. by C. Archer and J. S. Scott. New York: Knopf, 1923.

The Burning Bush. Trans. by Arthur G. Chater. New York: Knopf, 1932.

The Cross. Trans. by C. Archer. New York: Knopf, 1927.

Faithful Wife. Trans. by Arthur G. Chater. New York: Knopf, 1937.

Four Stories. Trans. by Naomi Walford. New York: Knopf, 1959.

Gunnar's Daughter. Trans. by Arthur G. Chater. New York: Knopf, 1936.

Ida Elizabeth. Trans. by Arthur G. Chater. New York: Knopf, 1933.

Images in a Mirror. Trans. by Arthur G. Chater. New York: Knopf, 1938.

In the Wilderness. Trans. Arthur G. Chater. New York: Knopf, 1929.

Jenny. Trans. by W. Emmé. New York: Knopf, 1921.

Kristin Lavransdatter. See translators of the individual volumes. New York: Knopf, 1929.

The Longest Years. Trans. by Arthur G. Chater. New York: Knopf, 1935.

Madame Dorothea. Trans. by Arthur G. Chater. New York: Knopf, 1940.

The Mistress of Husaby. Trans. by C. Archer. New York: Knopf, 1925.

The Snake Pit. Trans. by Arthur G. Chater. New York: Knopf, 1929.

Son Avenger. Trans. by Arthur G. Chater. New York: Knopf, 1930.

The Wild Orchid. Trans. by Arthur G. Chater. New York: Knopf, 1931.

BOOKS

540. Bayerschmidt, Carl F. Sigrid Undset. New York: Twayne, 1970.

This critical biography is largely a chronologically-arranged discussion of the works of Sigrid Undset. The author recognizes most of the strongest influences upon her work, particularly her fervent Christianity, which is shown to pervade the majority of her writing.

541. Sigrid Undset; Distinguished Author and Winner in 1928 of the Nobel Prize for Literature. New York: Knopf, 1932.

542. Vinde, Victor. Sigrid Undset, a Nordic Moralist. Seattle, Wash.: University of Washington Book Store, 1930.

Vinde negates any contention that Undset's Christianity makes an impact on her work, except in the recognition that man is a sinner who can never know happiness. Vinde sees only a purgatorial existence for man exhibited in the fiction of Sigrid Undset. This minimizes the importance of Undset's religious beliefs which is considerable.

543. Winsnes, Andreas Hofgaard. Sigrid Undset, a Study in Christian Realism. Tran. P. G. Foote. New York: Sheed & Ward, 1953.

This book maintains that Undset is a Christian Realist. At times this realism takes on a seemingly anti-romantic character. An emersion in the everyday world is evident in all her novels. Winsnes refers to Undset as one of the few great twentieth-century writers, because of the success of Undset within the context of the fictional worlds, both modern and medieval, that she creates.

DISSERTATIONS

544. Dunn, Margaret Mary. "Sigrid Undset's Two Novel-Cycles of Religious Conversion." Diss. Fordham University, 1966.

545. Kelly, Mary Berchans. "Sigrid Undset, Her Spiritual Development as Revealed in Her Novels." Diss. St. John's University, 1956.

546. Ruch, Velma Naomi. "Sigrid Undset's Kristin Lavransdatter: A Study of Its Literary Art and Its Reception in America, England, and Scandinavia." Diss. University of Wisconsin at Madison, 1957.

CHAPTERS AND MATERIALS IN BOOKS

547. Allen, W. Gore. "The Catholic: Sigrid Undset--Medieval." In Renaissance in the North. New York: Sheed & Ward, 1946, pp. 37-45.

This is a study of the influence of Catholicism on Undset's works, particularly her medieval epic tales, Kristin Lavransdatter and The Master of Hesviken. Allen postulates that perhaps Undset was initially drawn to Catholicism through her extensive study of the Middle Ages.

548. ________. "The Catholic: Sigrid Undset-- Modern." In Renaissance in the North. New York: Sheed & Ward, 1946, pp. 49-59.

A continuation of Allen's study of Undset, this section deals with her novels which have contemporary settings. He cites Images in a Mirror as a successful post-conversion novel because it goes far beyond religious propaganda while encompassing Undset's new-found beliefs.

549. Bach, Giovanni. "Norwegian Literature." In A History of the Scandinavian Literatures. Trans. and ed. Frederika Blankner. New York: Dial, 1938, pp. 68-70.

550. Beach, Joseph Warren. "Variations: Sigrid Undset." In Twentieth Century Novel: Studies in Technique. New York: Appleton-Century, 1932, pp. 263-72.

551. Drake, William A. "Sigrid Undset." In Contemporary European Writers. New York: Day, 1928, pp. 72-9.

Drake states that Undset's historical novels comprise her most successful writing. He recognizes as the most valuable quality of her writing her vivid portraits of her women characters, which, he says, are unique in their depth.

552. Gustafson, Alrik. "Christian Ethics in a Pagan World; Sigrid Undset." In Six Scandinavian Novelists. New York: Princeton University Press, 1940, pp. 286-361.

Gustafson strikes a comparison between Undset and George Eliot. The two share a similar moral sense and a sympathy for fallible humanity. Undset's emphasis, however, is on the characters of her novels. Gustafson says that the settings are full but subordinate to the people.

553. Marble, Annie Russell. "Sigrid Undset: Novelist of Medieval Norway and Ageless Humanity." In Nobel Prize Winners in Literature, 1901-1931. New York: Appleton-Century, 1932, pp. 327-45.

Marble presents a brief biographical sketch of Undset. She states that Undset is at her best in the historical novels and that the novels set in contemporary times are not found to be as personally satisfying.

554. Monroe, Nellie Elizabeth. "Art and Ideas in Sigrid Undset." In Novel and Society: A Critical Study of the Novel. Chapel Hill, N. C.: University of North Carolina Press, 1941, pp. 39-87.
Monroe points out some criticisms of Undset, among which is the charge that she is too sensory a novelist. Monroe is of the opinion that this is a mark in her favor, particularly in her attempts to evoke spiritualism.

555. Slochower, Harry. "Esthetic Confession." In No Voice Is Wholly Lost. London: Dennis Dobson, Ltd., 1946, pp. 134-7.
Slochower, like many other critics, focuses on Undset's Catholicism, particularly in relation to the reading of Kristin Lavransdatter. He sees Undset raising a number of questions in this epic which are opposed to tradition.

556. ________. "Feudal Socialism: Sigrid Undset's Kristin Lavransdatter." In Three Ways of Modern Man. New York: International Pubs., 1938, pp. 25-49.
Slochower focuses his attention almost entirely on Kristin Lavransdatter. He points out the modern aspects in the midst of the medieval setting. He also notes a kind of collectivism in her novel which is somewhat more akin to Catholicism than to Protestantism.

557. Van Gelder, Robert. "Sigrid Undset Speaks of Writing and War." In Writers and Writing. New York: Scribner's, 1946, pp. 108-10.
Van Gelder presents in Undset's own words some of her views on World War II, particularly the Nazi invasion of her homeland, and its effects on her writing.

CRITICAL ARTICLES

558. Allen, W. Gore. "Sigrid Undset: A New Judgment." Wind and the Rain 7 (1951), 157-65.

559. Beck, Richard. "Sigrid Undset and Her Novels on Medieval Life." Books Abroad 24, i(1950), 4-10.

560. Brady, Charles A. "An Appendix to the Sigridssaga." Thought 40 (Spring, 1965), 73-130.

Brady studies the sources used by Undset for her historical novels in an effort to understand the world she creates. He includes two previously unpublished letters by the author.

561. Bull, Francis. "Sigrid Undset." Samtiden 66 (1955), 269-80.

562. Ciklamini, Marlene. "Sigrid Undset's Letter to Hope Emily Allen." Journal of the Rutgers University Library 33, i (1969), 20-7.

563. Delaney, James D. "Visit to Sigrid Undset's Home." America, 5 April 1958, pp. 15-7.

564. Dunn, Margaret Mary. "The Master of Hestviken: A New Reading." Scandinavian Studies 38 (November, 1966), 281-94.

Dunn concerns herself only with volumes one and two of The Master of Hestviken in this study. This is an attempt to view Christian ideals and literary structure together in a work of art.

565. ________. "The Master of Hestviken: A New Reading II." Scandinavian Studies 40 (August, 1968), 210-24.

In this article Dunn continues her examination of The Master of Hestviken, studying the last two volumes of the tetralogy. She makes some comparisons between Undset's work and T. S. Eliot's The Four Quartets.

566. "Free Spirit of the North." American-Scandinavian Review 29 (March, 1941), 53-5.

567. Gerhart, M. "Kristin Lavransdatter." Journal of the American Academy of Religion 45 (1977), 309.

568. Kielland, E. "Three Essays on the Church of Norway in the Middle Ages." American-Scandinavian Review 27 (December, 1939), 337-40.

569. LaRosa, Barbara. "The Shock of Simplicity." Renascence 12 (Spring, 1960), 163-4.

570. Larsen, Hanna Astrup. "Four Scandinavian Feminists." Yale Review n. s. 5 (January, 1916), 347-62.

571. McCarthy, Colman. "Sigrid Undset." Critic 32 (January, 1974), 58-64.
The journalist Colman McCarthy has prepared a biographical sketch in praise of Undset and her accomplishments on the twenty-fifth anniversary of her death.

572. Monroe, Nellie Elizabeth. "Technique in Undset's Medieval Novels." Renascence 4 (Autumn, 1951), 53-7.
Monroe bases her study on the assumption that Undset's greatness as a writer depends on her technique rather than on her subject matter. This is a difficult thesis to prove given the epic proportions of the themes of Undset's novels. Monroe cites Undset's use of the Christian revelation and its effects on her characters.

573. "Norway and Norwegian Americans." Common Ground 2, iii(1942), 73-6.

574. Reedy, George C. "The Master of Hestviken." America, 1-8 July 1978, p. 17.

575. Rogers, B. J. "The Divine Disappointment of Kristin Lavransdatter." Cithara 2 (1962), 44-8.

576. Salomon, Richard. "The Future of Intellectual Germany: Jaspers vs. Undset." Kenyon Review 8 (Summer, 1946), 484-7.

577. "Transplanted Writers." Books Abroad 16 (October, 1942), 388.

578. Wallenstein, H. "Diary of an Adolescent." Family 19 (July, 1937), 176-7.

BOOK REVIEWS

The Axe

579. "The Axe." Booklist 24 (May, 1928), 323.

580. "The Axe." Boston Transcript, 11 February 1928, p. 2.

581. "The Axe." Cleveland Open Shelf, November 1928, p. 122.

582. "The Axe." New Republic, 20 June 1928, p. 130.

583. "The Axe." New York Times Book Review, 5 February 1928, p. 6.

584. "The Axe." Outlook, 7 March 1928, p. 398.

585. "The Axe." Pittsburgh Monthly Bulletin 33 (April, 1928), 194.

586. "The Axe." Pratt Institute Quarterly, Autumn 1928, p. 45.

587. "The Axe." World Tomorrow 11 (October, 1928), 426.

588. Blundell, Edmund. "The Axe." Nation and Athenaeum, 10 March 1928, p. 852.

589. Fadiman, C. P. "The Axe." New York Evening Post, 17 March 1928, p. 12.

590. Lohrke, Eugene. "The Axe." New York Herald-Tribune Books, 12 February 1928, p. 3.
Lohrke notes that the action, even the violent action, of the novel is related simply and calmly by Undset. He praises Chater's translation.

591. Parsons, A. B. "The Axe." Bookman 67 (April, 1928), 213.

592. Stork, W. "The Axe." Saturday Review of Literature, 2 June 1928, p. 930.
Stork praises Undset's portrayal of medieval life, the customs and laws. He adds that the reader can become immersed in the age.

593. Suckow, Ruth. "The Axe." New York World, 12 February 1928, p. 10m.

594. Thomas, Gilbert. "The Axe." Spectator, 10 March 1928, p. 393.

The Bridal Wreath

595. Bjorkman, Edwin. "The Bridal Wreath." Literary Review of the New York Evening Post, 21 April 1923, p. 624.

596. "The Bridal Wreath." Booklist 19 (July, 1923), 322.

597. "The Bridal Wreath." Boston Transcript, 28 April 1923, p. 5.

598. "The Bridal Wreath." Cleveland Open Shelf, September 1923, p. 67.

599. "The Bridal Wreath." Nation, 22 August 1923, p. 200.

600. "The Bridal Wreath." New York Times Book Review, 25 March 1923, p. 9.

The reviewer states that the novel captures the universal aspects of emotion and impulse, and that it is "well-written, well-constructed."

601. "The Bridal Wreath." Springfield Republican, 20 May 1923, p. 7a.

602. "The Bridal Wreath." The Times (London) Literary Supplement, 14 December 1923, p. 840.

603. Douglas, A. D. "The Bridal Wreath." New York Tribune, 25 March 1923, p. 22.

604. Larsen, Hanna Astrup. "The Bridal Wreath." Literary Digest International Book Review, March 1923, p. 32.

Larsen calls the novel "an epic of womanhood," powerfully told. She says that the novel and the author can be highly praised.

605. Stagg, Hunter. "Review of The Bridal Wreath." Reviewer 3 (April, 1023), 873-3.

The Burning Bush

606. Bentley, Phyllis. "The Burning Bush." New Statesman and Nation, 15 October 1932, p. 452.

Bentley praises the vitality of the book and the imaginative quality and magnificence of the landscape. She does, however, find Paul and his family unattractive characters.

607. Brande, Dorothea. "The Burning Bush." Bookman 75 (August, 1932), 405.

608. "The Burning Bush." Booklist 29 (September, 1932), 19.

609. "The Burning Bush." Boston Transcript, 31 August 1932, p. 2.

610. "The Burning Bush." Catholic World 136 (October, 1932), 115.

611. "The Burning Bush." Cleveland Open Shelf, July 1932, p. 16.

612. "The Burning Bush." New Republic, 14 September 1932, p. 134.

613. "The Burning Bush." Pittsburgh Monthly Bulletin 37 (October, 1932), 60.

614. "The Burning Bush." Pratt Institute Quarterly, Winter 1933, p. 37.

615. Cantwell, Robert. "The Burning Bush." Nation, 21 September 1932, p. 263.

Cantwell claims that the novel is extremely tedious and overly long. He also finds it repetitious of The Wild Orchid.

616. Carleton, P. D. "The Burning Bush." Saturday Review of Literature, 3 September 1932, p. 77.

617. Kolars, Mary. "The Burning Bush." Commonweal, 21 September 1932, p. 492.

Kolars calls The Burning Bush a "beautiful book, full of illumined and touching truths about men and women." She says the characterizations are full.

618. Kronenberger, Louis. "The Burning Bush." New York Times Book Review, 21 August 1932, p. 6.

619. Strong, L. A. G. "The Burning Bush." Spectator, 15 October 1932, p. 492.

620. Walton, E. L. "The Burning Bush." New York Herald-Tribune Books, 14 August 1932, p. 1.

The Cross

621. "The Cross." Booklist 23 (April, 1927), 312.

622. "The Cross." Cleveland Open Shelf, July 1927, p. 88.

623. "The Cross." Nation, 8 June 1927, p. 649.

624. "The Cross." New York Times Book Review, 20 February 1927, p. 8.
The reviewer has high praise for Undset--her romanticism, her mystical strain, her humanism, and her vivid backgrounds.

625. "The Cross." Pittsburgh Monthly Bulletin 32 (June, 1927), 289.

626. "The Cross." The Times (London) Literary Supplement, 28 April 1928, p. 300.

627. "The Cross." Wisconsin Library Bulletin 23 (May, 1927), 141.

628. Gulliver, Lucille. "The Cross." Boston Transcript, 19 February 1927, p. 5.

629. Hillyer, Robert. "The Cross." New Republic, 8 June 1927, p. 79.

630. Latimer, Margery. "The Cross." New York World, 3 April 1927, p. 13m.

631. Suckow, Ruth. "The Cross." New York Herald-Tribune Books, 28 March 1927, p. 2.
Suckow says that The Cross lacks some of the lyric passion of the first two volumes of Kristin Lavransdatter, but none of the emotional power. As such it is a fitting conclusion to the trilogy.

Faithful Wife

632. Canby, H. S. "Faithful Wife." Saturday Review of Literature, 9 October 1937, p. 6.

633. "Faithful Wife." Booklist, 15 November 1937, p. 108.

634. "Faithful Wife." Catholic World 146 (December, 1937), 371.

The reviewer says that Faithful Wife is Undset's weakest book, primarily because of its lack of direction. The translation by Chater is also said to be poor.

635. "Faithful Wife." Chicago Daily Tribune, 8 October 1938, p. 17.

636. "Faithful Wife." Christian Science Monitor, 27 October 1937, p. 10.

637. "Faithful Wife." Cleveland Open Shelf, November 1937, p. 24.

638. "Faithful Wife." Springfield Republican, 3 October 1937, p. 7e.

639. "Faithful Wife." Time, 25 October 1937, p. 80.

640. "Faithful Wife." The Times (London) Literary Supplement, 30 October 1937, p. 802.

641. Gibson, Wilfred. "Faithful Wife." Manchester Guardian , 2 November 1937, p. 7.

642. Owens, Olga. "Faithful Wife." Boston Transcript, 9 October 1937, p. 1.

643. Repplier, Agnes. "Faithful Wife." Commonweal, 12 November 1937, p. 79.

644. Rugoff, Milton. "Faithful Wife." New York Herald-Tribune Books, 3 October 1937, p. 5.

645. Walton, E. L. "Faithful Wife." Nation, 30 October 1937, p. 481.
Walton praises Undset's skill and calls the book "a very careful and subtle analysis of a modern woman functioning intelligently in an emotional crisis."

646. Young, Stanley. "Faithful Wife." New York Times Book Review, 10 October 1937, p. 1.

Four Stories

647. Burnette, Francis. "Four Stories." Library Journal, 15 June 1959, p. 2081.

648. Butcher, Fanny. "Four Stories." Chicago Sunday Tribune, 12 April 1959, p. 4.

649. "Four Stories." Booklist, 1 May 1959, p. 478.

650. "Four Stories." Bookmark 18 (May, 1959), 204.

651. "Four Stories." New Yorker, 27 June 1959, p. 90.

652. "Four Stories." Time, 1 June 1959, p. 92.

653. Hughes, Riley. "Four Stories." Catholic World 189 (July, 1959), 323.
Hughes states that these stories prove that Undset was as adept at writing stories about the twentieth century as about the medieval world.

654. Maddocks, Melvin. "Four Stories." Christian Science Monitor, 21 May 1959, p. 13.

655. Meras, Phyllis. "Four Stories." New York Herald-Tribune Books, 12 April 1959, p. 5.

656. Peden, William. "Four Stories." New York Times Book Review, 12 April 1959, p. 5.

657. Sansom, William. "Four Stories." Saturday Review of Literature, 18 April 1959, p. 50.
Sansom says the stories are masterpieces and compares Undset to James Joyce and Katherine Mansfield.

658. Stella, Sister Maris. "Four Stories." Commonweal, 21 February 1960, p. 602.

659. Stilwell, Robert L. "Review of Four Stories." Shenandoah 11 (Autumn, 1959), 37-9.

660. Voiles, Jane. "Four Stories." San Francisco Chronicle, 10 May 1959, p. 24.

Gunnar's Daughter

661. Butcher, Fanny. "Gunnar's Daughter." Chicago Daily Tribune, 25 July 1936, p. 8.

662. Brunini, J. C. "Gunnar's Daughter." Commonweal, 11 September 1936, p. 469.

663. Davenport, Basil. "Gunnar's Daughter." Saturday Review of Literature, 25 July 1936, p. 7.

664. "Gunnar's Daughter." Booklist 33 (October, 1936), 54.

665. "Gunnar's Daughter." Catholic World 143 (September, 1936), 763.

666. "Gunnar's Daughter." Christian Science Monitor, 12 August 1936, p. 11.

667. "Gunnar's Daughter." New Republic, 12 August 1936, p. 27.

668. "Gunnar's Daughter." Pratt Institute Quarterly, Autumn 1936, p. 41.

669. "Gunnar's Daughter." Springfield Republican, 30 August 1936, p. 7e.

670. "Gunnar's Daughter." Time, 27 July 1936, p. 58.

671. "Gunnar's Daughter." The Times (London) Literary Supplement, 7 November 1936, p. 905.
This reviewer says that Undset has managed to tell a tale in the tradition of the saga from a woman's point of view, filling in areas that the sagas neglect.

672. Kazin, Alfred. "Gunnar's Daughter." New York Herald-Tribune Books, 26 July 1936, p. 2.

673. Kronenberger, Louis. "Gunnar's Daughter." New York Times Book Review, 26 July 1936, p. 1.

674. Lester, T. S. "Gunnar's Daughter." Boston Transcript, 25 July 1936, p. 3.
Lester notes how the tale is simply told and objective in its treatment. The action of the novel is best related in simple terms.

675. Marriott, Charles. "Gunnar's Daughter." Manchester Guardian, 25 September 1936, p. 7.

676. Van Doren, Mark. "Gunnar's Daughter." Nation, 1 August 1936, p. 135.

Ida Elizabeth

677. Brickell, Herschel. "Ida Elizabeth." North American Review 136 (December, 1933), 569.

678. Carleton, P. D. "Ida Elizabeth." Saturday Review of Literature, 7 October 1933, p. 161.

679. Hutchison, Percy. "Ida Elizabeth." New York Times Book Review, 1 October 1933, p. 1.

680. "Ida Elizabeth." Booklist 30 (November, 1933), 80.

681. "Ida Elizabeth." Catholic World 138 (November, 1933), 240.

The reviewer states that, although the characterizations are good and the story is well told, the novel is "inconclusive and irritating" and some passages are "arid and boresome."

682. "Ida Elizabeth." Christian Science Monitor, 14 October 1933, p. 8.

683. "Ida Elizabeth." Cleveland Open Shelf, December 1933, p. 16.

684. "Ida Elizabeth." Nation, 6 December 1933, p. 660.

685. "Ida Elizabeth." New Republic, 6 December 1933, p. 112.

686. "Ida Elizabeth." Pratt Institute Quarterly, Winter 1934, p. 37.

687. "Ida Elizabeth." The Times (London) Literary Supplement, 21 December 1933, p. 908.

688. Mann, D. L. "Ida Elizabeth." Boston Transcript, 14 October 1933, p. 1.

689. Olson, A. L. "Ida Elizabeth." New York Times Book Review, 15 January 1933, p. 8.

690. Quennell, Peter. "Ida Elizabeth." New Statesman and Nation, 21 October 1933, p. 486.

Quennell also praises Undset's literary talents, but finds fault with the novel inasmuch as the novel is a bit too realistic in his opinion and that it concerns itself with trivialities.

691. Walton, E. L. "Ida Elizabeth." New York Herald-Tribune Books, 1 October 1933, p. 2.
Walton says that the greatest aspect of this novel is the character of Ida Elizabeth. The novel presents a fully imagined and depicted world.

Images in a Mirror

692. Beresford, J. D. "Images in a Mirror." Manchester Guardian, 16 September 1938, p. 5.

693. Davis, Elmer. "Images in a Mirror." Saturday Review of Literature, 27 August 1938, p. 5.
Davis says the book may be found discouraging by young readers. He states that it is really about the human condition, with no apologies added.

694. "Images in a Mirror." Booklist, 15 September 1938, p. 25.

695. "Images in a Mirror." Catholic World 148 (October, 1938), 123.

696. "Images in a Mirror." Christian Science Monitor, 7 September 1938, p. 11.

697. "Images in a Mirror." Cleveland Open Shelf, September 1938, p. 16.

698. "Images in a Mirror." New Republic, 31 August 1938, p. 112.

699. "Images in a Mirror." New Yorker, 27 August 1938, p. 66.

700. "Images in a Mirror." Pratt Institute Quarterly, Winter 1939, p. 36.

701. "Images in a Mirror." Springfield Republican, 11 September 1938, p. 7e.

702. "Images in a Mirror." The Times (London) Literary Supplement, 3 September 1938, p. 571.

703. Repplier, Agnes. "Images in a Mirror." Commonweal, 21 October 1938, p. 679.

704. Ross, Mary. "Images in a Mirror." New York Herald-Tribune Books, 21 August 1938, p. 2.

Ross states that the novel, though written twenty years prior to the reviewing date, does not seem at all dated. She also praises the characterizations of both men and women.

705. Salomon, L. B. "Images in a Mirror." Nation, 24 September 1938, p. 303.

706. Thompson, Ralph. "Images in a Mirror." Yale Review n. s. 28 (Autumn, 1938), xii.

Thompson is of the opinion that this is one of Undset's minor novels, and that it might have been shallow were it not for Undset's skillful hand.

707. Young, Stanley. "Images in a Mirror." New York Times Book Review, 21 August 1938, p. 6.

In the Wilderness

708. Douglas, Donald. "In the Wilderness." New York Herald-Tribune Books, 6 October 1929, p. 4.

709. "In the Wilderness." Booklist 26 (December, 1929), 121.

710. "In the Wilderness." Yale Review n. s. 19 (Winter, 1930), viii.

711. Irvine, L. L. "In the Wilderness." Nation and Athenaeum, 26 October 1929, p. 143.

712. Kronenberger, Louis. "In the Wilderness." New York Times Book Review, 13 October 1929, p. 9.
Kronenberger points out that this, the third volume of The Master of Hestviken, is full of life that transcends time. He notes that Undset never lets the book become picturesque.

713. Luhrs, Marie. "In the Wilderness." New York World, 20 October 1929, p. 11m.
Luhrs notes that In the Wilderness blends well with the other volumes of the tetralogy, with smooth transition. She says there are aspects of the modern in the midst of the medieval.

714. Robbins, F. L. "In the Wilderness." Outlook and Independent, 2 October 1929, p. 187.

Jenny

715. "Jenny." Freeman, 5 October 1921, p. 94.

716. "Jenny." Literary Review of the New York Evening Post, 2 July 1921, p. 11.

717. "Jenny." New York Times Book Review, 3 July 1921, p. 21.

718. Mann, D. L. "Jenny." Boston Transcript, 27 August 1921, p. 5.
Mann says that the novel provokes a number of questions, but sees this provocative nature as an attribute.

719. Toksvig, Signe. "Jenny." New Republic, 5 October 1921, p. 167.
Toksvig sees flashes of artistic ability in Jenny, but thinks the novel too rigid and gloomy to be highly recommended.

Kristin Lavransdatter

720. Bazarov, Konstantin. "Kristin Lavransdatter." Books and Bookmen 23 (January, 1978), 37.

721. Breslin, John J., S. J. "Kristin Lavransdatter." America, 12 February 1972, p. 155.

722. "Kristin Lavransdatter." Human Events, 25 November 1978, p. 11.

723. "Kristin Lavransdatter." Kliatt Paperback Book Guide 13 (January, 1979), 16.

724. "Kristin Lavransdatter." New York Times Book Review, 28 January 1979, p. 37.

725. Merriam, Doris F. "Kristin Lavransdatter." Frontier and Midland 9 (May, 1929), 363-5.

For additional reviews of Kristin Lavransdatter, see citations for the individual volumes of the trilogy: The Bridal Wreath, The Mistress of Husaby, and The Cross.

The Longest Years

726. Butcher, Fanny. "The Longest Years." Chicago Daily Tribune, 2 November 1935, p. 20.

727. Colgate, Miriam. "The Longest Years." American Review 6 (January, 1936), 374.

728. Kolars, Mary. "The Longest Years." Commonweal, 15 November 1935, p. 79.

729. Kronenberger, Louis. "The Longest Years." New York Times Book Review, 27 October 1935, p. 2.
Kronenberger says that this is a good, but not a great, book. He states that it is pleasant and that its insights are "sound, but seldom deep."

730. "The Longest Years." Booklist 32 (February, 1936), 170.

731. "The Longest Years." Catholic World 142 (January, 1936), 507.

732. "The Longest Years." Cleveland Open Shelf, October 1935, p. 20.

733. "The Longest Years." New Republic, 1 January 1936, p. 235.
The reviewer says that Undset has failed to endow this novel with the power to make the reader feel as though he were reliving the events.

734. "The Longest Years." Springfield Republican, 25 December 1935, p. 12.

735. Loveman, Amy. "The Longest Years." Saturday Review of Literature, 26 October 1935, p. 13.

736. Mann, D. L. "The Longest Years." Boston Transcript, 26 October 1935, p. 1.
Mann admires the book (which is based on incidents in Undset's own life) for its insight into Undset's background and into the child's reactions to her environment.

737. Quennell, Peter. "The Longest Years." New Statesman and Athenaeum, 16 November 1935, p. 746.

738. Ross, Mary. "The Longest Years." New York Herald-Tribune Books, 27 October 1935, p. 6.

739. Rugg, W. K. "The Longest Years." Christian Science Monitor, 6 November 1935, p. 12.

Madame Dorothea

740. Bullock, F. H. "Madame Dorothea." New York Herald-Tribune Books, 4 August 1940, p. 3.
Bullock states that Undset's works, Madame Dorothea included, present the continuity of time and of human nature.

741. Cordell, R. A. "Madame Dorothea." Saturday Review of Literature, 3 August 1940, p. 7.

742. Drew, Elizabeth. "Madame Dorothea." Atlantic Monthly 166 (September, 1940), n. p.

743. Gannett, Lewis. "Madame Dorothea." Boston Transcript, 1 August 1940, p. 11.

744. Graham, A. L. "Madame Dorothea." Library Journal 65 (August, 1940), 653.

745. Kronenberger, Louis. "Madame Dorothea." New York Times Book Review, 4 August 1940, p. 6.
Kronenberger praises Madame Dorothea for the story-telling and for the world it creates, but he states that the novel seems to be incomplete.

746. "Madame Dorothea." Booklist, 1 October 1940, p. 37.

747. "Madame Dorothea." Boston Transcript, 19 August 1940, p. 2.

748. "Madame Dorothea." Catholic World 152 (October, 1940), 117.
The reviewer does not recommend Madame Dorothea, for reasons of the "clinical frankness" of an abortion and of "adolescent passion run amuck."

749. "Madame Dorothea." Cleveland Open Shelf, July 1940, p. 10.

750. "Madame Dorothea." New Republic, 19 August 1940, p. 254.

751. "Madame Dorothea." New Yorker, 3 August 1940, p. 56.

752. "Madame Dorothea." Springfield Republican, 18 August 1940, p. 7e.

753. "Madame Dorothea." Time, 5 August 1940, p. 69.

754. Salomon, L. B. "Madame Dorothea." Nation, 10 August 1940, p. 117.

The Master of Hestviken

For reviews of The Master of Hestviken, see citations for the individual volumes of the tetralogy: The Axe, The Snake Pit, In the Wilderness, and The Son Avenger.

The Mistress of Husaby

755. Douglas, Donald. "The Mistress of Husaby." Nation, 5 August 1925, p. 170.

756. Kennedy, P. C. "The Mistress of Husaby." New Statesman, 10 October 1925, p. 728.

757. "The Mistress of Husaby." Booklist 21 (July, 1925), 385.

758. "The Mistress of Husaby." Cleveland Open Shelf, July 1925, p. 82.
The reviewer says that this book can be read independently of the first volume of the trilogy. He says, however, that it becomes tedious when it comes to the matter of political intrigue.

759. "The Mistress of Husaby." Nation and Athenaeum, 29 August 1925, p. 653.

760. "The Mistress of Husaby." New York Times Book Review, 19 May 1925, p. 17.

761. "The Mistress of Husaby." The Times (London) Literary Supplement, 3 September 1925, p. 570.
The reviewer has extremely high praise for the translation, which he says is virtually on a par with the original.

762. Paterson, Isabel. "The Mistress of Husaby." New York Tribune, 31 May 1925, p. 10.
Paterson says that this is excellent historical fiction. It captures not just the setting but the ideas and emotions of the people.

763. Porterfield, A. W. "The Mistress of Husaby." Saturday Review of Literature, 11 July 1925, p. 908.

Sigurd and His Brave Companions

764. Becker, M. L. "Sigurd and His Brave Companions." New York Herald-Tribune Books, 14 November 1943, p. 10.

765. Bostwick, R. O. "Sigurd and His Brave Companions." Library Journal, 15 December 1943, p. 1051.

766. Buell, E. L. "Sigurd and His Brave Companions." New York Times Book Review, 12 December 1943, p. 7.
Buell praises the vigor and color with which the tale is told. Buell claims that it clearly envisions the world as it once was. He recommends the book for children.

767. Jordan, A. M. "Sigurd and His Brave Companions." Horn Book 20 (January, 1944), 41.

768. Masten, H. A. "Sigurd and His Brave Companions." Christian Science Monitor, 9 December 1943, p. 8.

769. "Sigurd and His Brave Companions." Booklist, 15 December 1943, p. 152.

770. "Sigurd and His Brave Companions." Catholic World 158 (December, 1943), 316.

771. "Sigurd and His Brave Companions." Commonweal, 19 November 1943, p. 119.

772. "Sigurd and His Brave Companions." New Yorker, 4 December 1943, p. 130.
The reviewer says that although the story has some distinction, it is not successful. He does not think it will satisfy young American readers.

Snake Pit

773. Brickell, Herschel. "Snake Pit." North American Review 227 (February, 1929), adv.

774. Carleton, P. D. "Snake Pit." Saturday Review of Literature, 13 April 1929, p. 878.
Carleton says that this is a tale well told. He claims that the saga style is brought into the twentieth century with great success.

775. Kronenberger, Louis. "Snake Pit." New York Times Book Review, 6 January 1929, p. 9.

776. Latimer, Margery. "Snake Pit." New York World, 3 March 1929, p. 11m.

777. McHugh, Vincent. "Snake Pit." New York Evening Post, 5 January 1929, p. 8m.

778. Parsons, A. B. "Snake Pit." Nation, 13 March 1929, p. 316.

779. Paterson, Isabel. "Snake Pit." New York Herald-Tribune Books, 6 January 1929, p. 1.

780. "Snake Pit." Booklist 25 (March, 1929), 248.

781. "Snake Pit." Catholic World 129 (May, 1929), 242.

782. "Snake Pit." Springfield Republican, 24 February 1929, p. 7e.

783. "Snake Pit." The Times (London) Literary Supplement, 30 May 1929, p. 434.
The reviewer praises accuracy and the depth of study of the time period and also the intricacy of the characterizations. The translation by Chateris also lauded.

Son Avenger

784. Douglas, Donald. "Son Avenger." New York Herald-Tribune Books, 14 September 1930, p. 2.
Douglas has high praise for Undset's ability to evoke the medieval world. He compares the end of the tetralogy to "Gotterdämmerung."

785. Kronenberger, Louis. "Son Avenger." New York Times Book Review, 21 September 1930, p. 7.

786. Lohrke, Eugene. "Son Avenger." Nation, 10 September 1930, p. 273.

787. MacAfee, Helen. "Son Avenger." Yale Review n. s. 20 (Autumn, 1930), x.

788. McHugh, Vincent. "Son Avenger." New York Evening Post, 1 September 1930, p. 55.

789. Mann, D. L. "Son Avenger." Boston Transcript, 4 October 1930, p. 1.

790. Pritchett, V. S. "Son Avenger." Spectator, 1 November 1930, p. 644.

791. Ross, V. P. "Son Avenger." Outlook and Independent, 24 September 1930, p. 146.

792. Simpson, Clinton. "Son Avenger." New York World, 19 October 1930, p. 3e.

793. "Son Avenger." Booklist 27 (December, 1930), 163.

794. "Son Avenger." Bookman 72 (October, 1930), 170.
The reviewer says that the realism of the novel fits in well with its theme and its location in history. He also finds Undset insightful.

795. "Son Avenger." Cleveland Open Shelf, November 1930, p. 143.

796. "Son Avenger." Pittsburgh Monthly Bulletin 35 (October, 1930), 71.

797. "Son Avenger." Pratt Institute Quarterly, Winter 1931, p. 39.

798. "Son Avenger." Saturday Review, 6 December 1930, p. 747.

799. Tomlinson, K. C. "Son Avenger." Nation and Athenaeum, 20 December 1930, p. 413.
Tomlinson says the book is too long and finds no stylistic differences or distinctions among Scandinavian novelists.

The Wild Orchid

800. Brande, Dorothea. "The Wild Orchid." Bookman 74 (December, 1931), 466.

801. Douglas, Donald. "The Wild Orchid." New York Herald-Tribune Books, 27 September 1931, p. 4.
Douglas admires the genius behind The Wild Orchid, but dislikes the manipulation of the characters for no apparent reason.

802. Kronenberger, Louis. "The Wild Orchid." New York Times Book Review, 27 September 1931, p. 5.

803. Meynell, Viola. "The Wild Orchid." New Statesman and Nation, 24 October 1931, p. 517.

804. Strong, L. A. G. "The Wild Orchid." Spectator, 10 October 1931, p. 478.

805. "The Wild Orchid." Booklist 28 (November, 1931), 100.

806. "The Wild Orchid." Boston Transcript, 25 November 1931, p. 2.

807. "The Wild Orchid." Cleveland Open Shelf, December 1931, p. 146.

808. "The Wild Orchid." Outlook and Independent, 7 October 1931, p. 185.

809. "The Wild Orchid." Pittsburgh Monthly Bulletin 36 (December, 1931), p. 84.

810. "The Wild Orchid." The Times (London) Literary Supplement, 22 October 1931, p. 818.
The reviewer praises the depiction of the Norwegian landscape, but finds fault with Paul's conversion to Catholicism. This appears to the reviewer to be propagandistic.

PÄR LAGERKVIST
1891-1974

Pär Lagerkvist was born on May 23, 1891, in Värjö in the province of Småland. He was the youngest of the seven children of Anders Johan and Johanna Blad Lagerkvist. Pär's parents and grandparents, like most of the residents of Värjö, were rather conservative and very religious. His father was employed at the railway station and the family lived above the station's restaurant.

As a young student in Värjö, Pär joined a radical group in reaction to the conservatism of the town. The members of the group called themselves the "Socialists of the Sixth Form." They normally held meetings when the rest of the townspeople were at church on Sunday mornings. They espoused Darwinism and sympathized with Strindberg's battle against the church.

After his graduation from the gymnasium at Värjö, he went to Uppsala University to study literature and art history. Pär apparently did not take to the university life; he stayed at Uppsala only one term. In 1913 he traveled to Paris and remained there three months. He took great interest in art, particularly in the cubist art of the period.

The idea of cubism fascinated him and influenced some of his writing. At this time Pär wrote reviews of modern fiction and published a critical work, Word Art and Picture Art. He was overwhelmed by avant-garde Paris, but was in some ways tied to his past. He could not entirely shake the conservative atmosphere in which he grew up, though he tried.

Throughout his writing career, Lagerkvist displayed a narrow range of subject matter but a great variety of literary technique. The shifts in emphasis and mood are particularly evident in his short fiction. Despite the shifts, a sense of continuity exists throughout his works. The technique he used most often in his shorter works was the fable. In his fables it is clear that he was a moralist, but it was not an orthodox morality. At times he used satire and parody to present his own brand of morality.

Through his early career Pär Lagerkvist confined his writing to short stories, novellas, poetry, and plays. His first novel, The Dwarf, was not published until 1944. With The Dwarf Lagerkvist created a best-seller. The novel's setting, Renaissance court life, acknowledged Lagerkvist's use of historic detail and enhanced the realism of the novel. The plot, symbolism and allusion notwithstanding, was eloquent in its simplicity. The story told, and the morality to which the reader was exposed, is the Dwarf's. The reliability of his telling was not always sound, but his viewpoint gave a consistency to the novel.

In 1951, Lagerkvist published Barabbas. It marked the beginning of a pentalogy which has the commonality of a Christian setting. Lagerkvist took Barabbas, a criminal barely mentioned in the Bible, and gave him a history, a personality, a life. Barabbas becomes involved in a quest for truth. In that quest Lagerkvist depicted the duality of man's nature, the admixture of good and evil. Barabbas seeks Christianity, but is rejected by the Christians. He is executed, and is separated from the Christians, even in death, and dies alone.

The same year Barabbas was published, Pär Lagerkvist received the Nobel Prize in literature. The award was given to him in recognition of a body of work that did not limit itself to one genre. He was well known for his poetry and his plays and was becoming well known for his fiction.

The second novel of his pentalogy is The Sibyl, published in 1956. At the time of its publication Walter Gustafson, in his article entitled "Sibyllan and the Patterns of Lagerkvist's Works," called it "the epitome of [Lagerkvist's] work, a summary, and a complete and daring culmination." In actuality it was not the culmination; three novels of the pentalogy remained to appear. The Sibyl again embodies Lagerkvist's idea of a quest for truth. It displays themes that run through virtually all of his writing. It includes Lagerkvist's vision of the basic difficulty of life: the simultaneous existence of opposites, the good and evil that exist within man.

Lagerkvist went back to his study of the cubist form, of the verbal thesis of what Picasso and Braque had been doing with visual art. That technique allowed Lagerkvist to express the duality of the characters' natures. Also, the form allowed him to arrive at no conclusion, only to depict the conflict. The novel itself was a search on the part of Lagerkvist.

The final three novels of the crucifixion pentalogy are closely related. In fact, they are considered by some to constitute a trilogy, though they resemble the previous two in technique, form, and theme. The three novels revolve around a single character, Tobias, a sort of Everyman. Tobias's struggles take him through periods of despair, doubt, and peacefulness that acknowledge the uncertainty of man's existence. His journey took him through The Death of Ahasuerus, The Holy Land, and Herod and Mariamne.

In all of Lagerkvist's works there is a speculation about religion. Though he disassociated himself from organized religion at an early age, he searched to see if the Christian ideals actually existed. None of his characters ever finds a clear answer and neither did Lagerkvist. His life was an integration of many opposites: quest for life, but fear of it; passion, yet intellectual asceticism; search for the supernatural, but rejection of dogma. Perhaps his most important contribution to literature was his experimentation with form, which influenced many writers in the first half of this century and which continues to fascinate scholars.

MAJOR WORKS IN ENGLISH

Barabbas. Trans. by Alan Blair. New York: Random House, 1951.

The Death of Ahasuerus. Trans. by Naomi Walford. New York: Random House, 1962.

The Dwarf. Trans. by Alexandra Dick [pseud.]. New York: L. B. Fischer, 1945.

The Eternal Smile and Other Stories. Trans. by Alan Blair and others. New York: Random House, 1954.

Herod and Mariamne. Trans. by Naomi Walford. New York: Knopf, 1968.

The Holy Land. Trans. by Naomi Walford. New York: Random House, 1966.

The Pilgrim at Sea. Trans. by Naomi Walford. New York: Random House, 1964.

The Sibyl. Trans. by Naomi Walford. New York: Random House, 1958.

BOOKS

811. Ryberg, Anders. Pär Lagerkvist in Translation: A Bibliography Compiled by Anders Ryberg. Stockholm: A. Bonnier's Boktryckeri, 1964.

812. Scobbie, Irene. Pär Lagerkvist: An Introduction. Stockholm: Swedish Institute, 1963.

813. Sjöberg, Leif. Pär Lagerkvist. New York: Columbia University Press, 1976.
Brief incidents from Lagerkvist's life are used to illustrate the evolution of his novels. Particularly pervasive in his writings and in his life are religious concerns. Sjöberg depicts Lagerkvist as being torn between modern science and a desire to cling to some traditional beliefs.

814. Spector, Robert Donald. Pär Lagerkvist. New York: Twayne, 1973.
Lagerkvist's experimentalism, his rebelliousness, are noted as having great effects on his writing. Although Spector also discusses Lagerkvist's poetry and drama, the central focus is on his fiction, and upon the preoccupation with religion (though not conventional religion) in his works.

815. Weathers, Winston. Pär Lagerkvist; a Critical Essay. Grand Rapids, Mich.: W. B. Eerdmans, 1968.
Weathers examines Lagerkvist and his work from an admittedly Christian perspective, which, though it recognizes the author's religious and moral preoccupation (dealing with archetypal rather than realistic figures), brings a bias into his examination and serves to obscure some of Lagerkvist's intentions.

CHAPTERS AND MATERIALS IN BOOKS

816. Bach, Giovanni. "Swedish Literature." In A History of the Scandinavian Literatures. Trans. and ed. Frederika Blankner. New York: Dial, 1938, p. 142.

817. Gustafson, Alrik. "Realism Renewed and Challenged." In A History of Swedish Literature. Minneapolis: University of Minnesota Press, 1961, pp. 392-407.

818. Spector, Robert Donald. "Lagerkvist's Dialogue of the Soul." In Scandinavian Studies: Essays Presented to Dr. Henry Goddard Leach. Ed Carl F. Bayerschmidt and Erik J. Friis. Seattle: University of Washington, 1945, pp. 302-10.
Concentrating on four novels, Barabbas, The Death of Ahasuerus, Pilgrim at Sea, and The Sibyl, Spector analyzes Lagerkvist's philosophy that the only reality for man is that which is evident at the moment.

CRITICAL ARTICLES

819. Ahlenius, Holger. "The Dramatic Work of Pär Lagerkvist." American-Scandinavian Review 28 (1940), 301-8.

820. Åhnebrink, L. "Pär Lagerkvist: A Seeker and a Humanist." Pacific Spectator 6 iv (1952), 400-12.

821. Baker, C. "Evening Land 1975." Theology Today 34 (1977), 108.

822. Benson, Adolph B. "Pär Lagerkvist: Nobel Laureate." College English 13 (May, 1952), 417-24.

823. Bloch, Adèle. "The Mythical Female in the Fictional Works of Pär Lagerkvist." International Fiction Review 1 (1974), 48-53.

824. Braybrooke, Neville. "Pär Lagerkvist." Catholic World 176 (January, 1953), 260.

825. Edfelt, Johannes. "Pär Lagerkvist." Norseman 10 (1952), 42-8.

826. Ellestad, Everett M. "Lagerkvist and Cubism: A Study of Theory and Practice." Scandinavian Studies 45 (Winter, 1973), 38-53.

Ellestad attempts to draw some parallels between literary and pictorial cubism and to explain Lagerkvist's experiments with literary cubism. His attention is focused solely upon the style and technique of Lagerkvist's writing.

827. Farber, Marjorie. "Review of The Dwarf." Kenyon Review 8 (Spring, 1946), 330-3.

Farber's analysis of The Dwarf is too detailed to be placed with other reviews of the book.

828. Flodstrom, Arthur. "'Ångest' and Cubism." Scandinavica 10 (1971), sup., 5-18.

Flodstrom maintains that Ångest is indebted to cubism, though it differs from Lagerkvist's earlier cubist novel, Motiv, in that it has progressed somewhat beyond cubism.

829. Gustafson, Alrik. "Pär Lagerkvist and Barabbas." American Swedish Monthly 45 (November, 1951), 11, 23, 25.

830. ________. "The Patterns of Art of Pär Lagerkvist." Edda 41 (1954), 346-50.

831. Gustafson, Walter W. "Pär Lagerkvist and Archaic Art." Scandinavian Studies 27 (Winter, 1955), 64-70.

832. Gustafson, Walter W. "Pär Lagerkvist and His Symbols." Books Abroad 26, i (1952), 20-3.

833. ________. "Sibyllan and the Patterns of Lagerkvist's Works." Scandinavian Studies 30 (Winter, 1958), 131-6.

834. Jackson, Naomi. "The Fragmented Mirror: Lagerkvist's The Dwarf." Discourse 8 (Spring, 1965), 185-93.

Jackson takes a Freudian look at Lagerkvist's characterizations in The Dwarf. She also sees the conflict between good and evil that is evident in Lagerkvist's fiction.

835. Johannesson, Eric O. "Pär Lagerkvist and the Art of Rebellion." Scandinavian Studies 30 (Winter, 1958), 19-29.

836. Kattsoff, Louis O. "Encounter with God in the Novellas of Pär Lagerkvist." Discourse 9 (Autumn, 1966), 378-88.

837. Kehl, D. G. "The Chiaroscuro World of Pär Lagerkvist." Modern Fiction Studies 15 (Summer, 1969), 241-50.

Kehl uses the Italian term chiaroscuro, which means light-dark, as a means of describing the many dualisms in Lagerkvist's work. He sees Lagerkvist as offering a possibility for light and life in the midst of darkness.

838. Linner, Sven. "Pär Lagerkvist's The Eternal Smile and The Sibyl." Scandinavian Studies 37 (May, 1965), 160-7.

In studying the two works, Linner determines that The Eternal Smile may be read either as being Christian or non-Christian, but The Sibyl represents a definite move away from the faith in which he was raised.

839. Malmström, Gunnel. "The Hidden God." Scandinavica 10 (1971), sup., 57-67.
According to Malmström, Lagerkvist's works represent a search for "the hidden God," not in the usual sense of the deity, but a search for solutions to the metaphysical problems of life.

840. Mjöberg, Jövan. "Pär Lagerkvist and the Ancient Greek Drama." Scandinavian Studies 25 (Winter, 1953), 46-51.

841. Nielson, Marion Louis. "Review of The Eternal Smile and Other Stories." Western Review 19 (Summer, 1955), 308-14.

842. Ohmann, Richard M. "Apostle of Uncertainty." Commonweal, 11 May 1962, pp. 170-2.

843. Ramsey, Roger. "Pär Lagerkvist: The Dwarf and Dogma." Mosaic 5 (Spring, 1972), 97-106.
Ramsey sees Bernardo as the moral center of The Dwarf. He notes that there are no answers to Bernardo's questions of the meaning of life. Ramsey says that Lagerkvist parodies the dogmas of the Church and the dogma of power.

844. Scobbie, Irene. "Contrasting Characters in Barabbas." Scandinavian Studies 32 (November, 1960), 212-20.
Scobbie concentrates on her exegesis of Barabbas rather than a search for the philosophical statement of the novel. She maintains that it is a well-written and well-constructed work rather than merely a pronouncement on religion.

845. ________. "An Interpretation of Lagerkvist's Mariamne." Scandinavian Studies 45 (Spring, 1973), 128-34.
In examining Mariamne, Scobbie points out the obvious conflict bewteen a pessimistic and an optimistic view of man. It is a seemingly desolate story, with just a shread of optimism.

846. Scobbie, Irene. "The Significance of Lagerkvist's 'Dwarf'." Scandinavica 10 (1971), sup., 35-43.

Scobbie sees the Dwarf in Lagerkvist's novel as a means by which the other characters (and the reader) can be made aware of what lies within one's own soul.

847. Sloman, Judith. "Existentialism in Pär Lagerkvist and Isaac Bashevis Singer." Minnesota Review 5 (August-October, 1965), 206-12.

Sloman equates God in Lagerkvist's novels with his metaphysical search, but does not clearly examine Lagerkvist's wish to break with the God of his parents.

848. Spector, Robert Donald. "The Dwarf: A Note on Lagerkvist's Use of Deformity." Modern Language Notes 70 (June, 1955), 432-3.

849. ________. "Lagerkvist and Existentialism." Scandinavian Studies 32 (November, 1960), 203-11.

Spector discusses some existential qualities of Lagerkvist's work. For example, a rebellion against the rationalism of classical thought and the reliance upon truth formed from subjectivity are evident. The Eternal Smile is cited as an excellent example of the existential in Lagerkvist.

850. ________. "Lagerkvist, Swift, and the Devices of Fantasy." Western Humanities Review 12 (Winter, 1958), 75-9.

The fantastic atmosphere of some of Lagerkvist's novels is studied by Spector. Spector notes that Lagerkvist uses fantasy as a means of revealing truth, but he also uses the detachment that accompanies fantasy.

851. ________. "Lagerkvist's Short Fiction." American-Scandinavian Review 57 (1969), 260-5.

852. Spector, Robert Donald. "Lagerkvist's Uses of Deformity." Scandinavian Studies 33 (November, 1961), 209-17.
Spector notes that deformity, particularly in The Eternal Smile, Barabbas, and The Dwarf, provides Lagerkvist with a means of symbolizing the morals and values present in man.

853. ________. "The Limbo World of Pär Lagerkvist." American-Scandinavian Review 43 (September, 1955), 271-4.

854. ________. "Structure and Meaning of The Eternal Smile." Modern Language Notes 71 (March, 1956) 206-7.

855. Sundén, Hjalmar. "Tobias's Pilgrimage." Scandinavica 10 (1971), sup., 69-80.
Sundén notes the possibility of comparison of Tobias (a central figure in several of Lagerkvist's novels in his crucifixion cycle) and Christian in Bunyan's The Pilgrim's Progress.

856. Swanson, Roy Arthur. "Evil and Love in Lagerkvist's Crucifixion Cycle." Scandinavian Studies 38 (November, 1966), 302-17.
Swanson points out an intermingling of love and evil in the crucifixion cycle of Lagerkvist. He sees Golgotha as the symbol for evil and Calvary as the symbol for love and notes an equation of the two as the cycle is completed.

857. ________. "Lagerkvist's Dwarf and the Redemption of Evil." Discourse 13 (Spring, 1970), 192-211.
Swanson examines the characterization of the dwarf in the novel of that name and also in other of Lagerkvist's works.

858. Vowles, Richard B. "The Fiction of Pär Lagerkvist." Western Humanities Review 8 (Spring, 1954), 111-7.
Lagerkvist's originality and vision are the subjects of Vowles' article. The vision is an obviously dark one with evil receiving more notice in Lagerkvist's novels than good.

859. Wills, A. "Review of 'Guest of Reality'." Life and Letters 15 (Winter, 1936), 198-9.

BOOK REVIEWS

Barabbas

860. "Barabbas." Booklist, 1 November 1951, p. 86.

861. "Barabbas." Bookmark 11 (December, 1951), 60.

862. "Barabbas." Kirkus, 1 August 1951, p. 409.

863. "Barabbas." New Yorker, 17 November 1951, p. 180.

864. "Barabbas." San Francisco Chronicle, 11 November 1951, p. 11.

865. "Barabbas." Time, 3 December 1951, p. 110.

866. "Barabbas." The Times (London) Literary Supplement, 14 March 1952, p. 185.
The reviewer praises the vividness of the Passion and the Crucifixion, and also Lagerkvist's conception of the character of Barabbas.

867. "Barabbas." Wisconsin Library Bulletin 48 (January, 1952), 37.

868. Bates, Graham. "Barabbas." Saturday Review of Literature, 27 October 1951, p. 12.

869. Breit, Harvey. "Barabbas." New York Times Book Review, 25 November 1951, p. 4.

870. Hughes, Riley. "Barabbas." Catholic World 174 (March, 1952), 468.

871. Jenkins, Elizabeth. "Barabbas." Manchester Guardian, 28 March 1952, p. 4.

872. Jones, Llewellyn. "Barabbas." New York Herald-Tribune Book Review, 14 October 1951, p. 7.
Jones says that the story is ambiguous and that it is an ambiguity of the twentieth century. Jones finds parallels between the time of Christ and this century.

873. King, Carlyle. "Barabbas." Canadian Forum 32 (June, 1952), 70.

874. Lean, Tangye. "Barabbas." Spectator, 4 April 1952, p. 460.

875. Lowry, Robert. "Barabbas." New York Times Book Review, 7 October 1951, p. 4.
Lowry compares Lagerkvist's prose style to Andre Gide's. He says that it is a style that highlights the religious conflict and the spiritual dilemma.

876. Raymond, John. "Barabbas." New Statesman and Nation, 15 March 1952, p. 326.

877. Rolo, C. J. "Barabbas." Atlantic Monthly 188 (December, 1951), 96.

878. Sullivan, Richard. "Barabbas." Chicago Sunday Tribune, 14 October 1951, p. 3.

879. Webster, H. C. "Barabbas." New Republic, 21 January 1952, p. 20.

The Death of Ahasuerus

880. Adams, Phoebe. "The Death of Ahasuerus." Atlantic Monthly 209 (May, 1962), 128.

881. Ascherson, Neal. "The Death of Ahasuerus." New Statesman, 11 May 1962, p. 684.

882. Bruns, J. E. "The Death of Ahasuerus." Catholic World 196 (November, 1962), 129.

883. Cruttwell, Patrick. "The Death of Ahasuerus." Guardian, 25 May 1962, p. 9.

884. "The Death of Ahasuerus." Booklist, 15 April 1962, p. 564.

885. "The Death of Ahasuerus." Christian Century, 18 April 1962, p. 492.

886. "The Death of Ahasuerus." Kirkus, 15 December 1961, p. 1092.

887. "The Death of Ahasuerus." Time, 23 February 1962, p. 104.

888. "The Death of Ahasuerus." The Times (London) Literary Supplement, 18 May 1962, p. 361.
While most reviewers praise The Death of Ahasuerus, this reviewer says it is "a silly and pointless little book."

889. Fuller, Edmund. "The Death of Ahasuerus." New York Times Book Review, 1 April 1962, p. 40.

890. Gentry, Curt. "The Death of Ahasuerus." San Francisco Chronicle, 4 March 1962, p. 24.

891. Lindgren, R. E. "The Death of Ahasuerus." Library Journal, 1 March 1962, p. 994.

892. Maddocks, Melvin. "The Death of Ahasuerus." Christian Science Monitor, 19 April 1962, p. 7.
Maddocks says this novel is insightful, especially in the religious possibilities implied by Lagerkvist.

893. Payne, Robert. "The Death of Ahasuerus." Saturday Review, 24 February 1962, p. 29.

894. Seidenspinner, Clarence. "The Death of Ahasuerus." Chicago Sunday Tribune, 18 February 1962, p. 4.

895. Spector, Robert Donald. "The Death of Ahasuerus." New York Herald-Tribune Book Review, 18 February 1962, p. 6.
Spector says that the book will be displeasing to readers expecting or hoping for a didactic statement or a clear narrative.

The Dwarf

896. Basso, Hamilton. "The Dwarf." New Yorker, 17 November 1945, p. 114.
Basso expresses his distaste for books that consciously attempt to be displeasing and adds The Dwarf to that body of writing.

897. Bullock, F. H. "The Dwarf." Book Week (Chicago Sun), 25 November 1945, p. 18.

898. Chubb, T. C. "The Dwarf." New York Times Book Review, 25 November 1945, p. 4.

899. "The Dwarf." Kirkus, 15 November 1945, p. 498.

900. "The Dwarf." Springfield Republican, 23 December 1945, p. 4d.

901. Kranz, H. B. "The Dwarf." Saturday Review of Literature, 1 December 1945, p. 74.
Kranz finds the novel admirable in its subtlety and beauty. His primary criticism is that The Dwarf is too short to learn enough about the characters.

The Eternal Smile and Other Stories

902. Brown, F. J. "The Eternal Smile and Other Stories." Books and Bookmen 16 (May, 1971), 54.

903. Cadogen, Lucy. "The Eternal Smile and Other Stories." New Statesman, 5 March 1971, p. 311.

904. Cooperman, Stanley. "The Eternal Smile and Other Stories." Nation, 31 July 1954, p. 94.

905. "The Eternal Smile and Other Stories." Best Sellers, 1 September 1971, p. 151.

906. "The Eternal Smile and Other Stories." Booklist, 15 July 1954, p. 451.

907. "Review of The Eternal Smile and Other Stories." Chicago Review 9 (Fall, 1955), 122.

908. "The Eternal Smile and Other Stories." Christian Science Monitor, 13 May 1971, p. 11.

909. "The Eternal Smile and Other Stories." Kirkus, 1 May 1954, p. 294.

910. "The Eternal Smile and Other Stories." Kirkus, 15 April 1971, p. 461.

911. "The Eternal Smile and Other Stories." New Yorker, 19 June 1954, p. 99.

912. "The Eternal Smile and Other Stories." Publishers Weekly, 26 April 1971, p. 61.

913. "The Eternal Smile and Other Stories." Time, 28 June 1954, p. 92.

914. "The Eternal Smile and Other Stories." Wisconsin Library Bulletin 50 (October, 1954), 210.

915. Fitzsimmons, Tom. "The Eternal Smile and Other Stories." New Republic, 12 July 1954, p. 18.

916. Harrison, W. K. "The Eternal Smile and Other Stories." Library Journal, 15 June 1954, p. 1225.

917. Hughes, Riley. "The Eternal Smile and Other Stories." Catholic World 150 (October, 1954), 73.

Hughes is of the opinion that the long stories are too long and the short stories are too short.

918. Johnson, Robert Dale. "The Eternal Smile and Other Stories." Library Journal, 15 June 1971, p. 2103.

919. Mercier, Vivian. "The Eternal Smile and Other Stories." Commonweal, 9 July 1954, p. 346.

920. Paulding, Gouverneur. "The Eternal Smile and Other Stories." New York Herald-Tribune Book Review, 13 June 1954, p. 5.

Paulding finds a couple of the stories disturbing, but he also finds passages of depth and insight in each of the tales.

921. Peden, William. "The Eternal Smile and Other Stories." Saturday Review, 10 July 1954, p. 13.

Peden sees the stories as affirmations of man's dignity and goodness, in spite of the dark and violent aspects of Lagerkvist's writing.

922. Pisko, E. S. "The Eternal Smile and Other Stories." Christian Science Monitor, 5 August 1954, p. 11.

923. Rolo, C. J. "The Eternal Smile and Other Stories." Atlantic Monthly 194 (August, 1954), 85.

924. Schorer, Mark. "The Eternal Smile and Other Stories." New York Times Book Review, 13 June 1954, p. 4.

925. Trotter, Stewart. "The Eternal Smile and Other Stories." Listener, 11 March 1971, p. 312.

926. Wagenknecht, Edward. "The Eternal Smile and Other Stories." Chicago Sunday Tribune, 20 June 1954, p. 3.

Herod and Mariamne

927. Adams, Phoebe. "Herod and Mariamne." Atlantic Monthly 222 (November, 1968), 144.

928. Heiney, Donald. "Herod and Mariamne." Christian Science Monitor, 31 October 1968, p. 9.
Heiney says that the novel has to be read like the Bible, with nothing taken at face value. He adds that there is little or nothing concrete about the book.

929. "Herod and Mariamne." Kirkus, 1 January 1968, p. 6.

930. "Herod and Mariamne." New Yorker, 26 April 1968, p. 170.

931. "Herod and Mariamne." Publishers Weekly, 5 August 1968, p. 53.

932. Hill, W. B. "Herod and Mariamne." America, 30 November 1968, p. 566.

933. ________. "Herod and Maramne." Best Sellers, 1 November 1968, p. 316.
Hill finds simplicity and eloquence in the brevity of the novel. There is no suspense, but Hill does not see this as a failing in any way.

934. Thompson, L. S. "Herod and Mariamne." Library Journal, 15 October 1968, p. 3799.

935. Weathers, Winston. "Herod and Mariamne." Commonweal, 10 January 1968, p. 478.

The Holy Land

936. Adams, Phoebe. "The Holy Land." Atlantic Monthly 217 (June, 1966), 138.

937. "The Holy Land." Booklist, 1 June 1966, p. 948.

938. "The Holy Land." Choice 3 (November, 1966), 778.

939. "The Holy Land." Kirkus, 1 March 1966, p. 361.

940. "The Holy Land." The Times (London) Literary Supplement, 28 April 1966, p. 361.

941. "The Holy Land." Virginia Quarterly Review 42 (Summer, 1966), xciv.

942. Lamott, K. "The Holy Land." Holiday 40 (November, 1966), 151.

943. Lindgren, R. E. "The Holy Land." Library Journal, 22 May 1966, p. 2363.
Lindgren recommends the book for its clear symbolism and for the skill of Lagerkvist's writing.

944. Lundbergh, Holger. "The Holy Land." New York Times Book Review, 22 May 1966, p. 5.

945. Maddocks, Melvin. "The Holy Land." Christian Science Monitor, 26 May 1966, p. 11.
Maddocks praises The Holy Land for its passion. He states that it may even be a disguised autobiography.

946. Morse, J. Mitchell. "Review of The Holy Land." Hudson Review 19 (Autumn, 1966), 507-14.

947. West, Paul. "The Holy Land." Book Week, 15 May 1966, p. 14.
West has a low opinion of The Holy Land. He states that it is "as shallow as the worst of Soviet propaganda."

The Marriage Feast

948. Ferrari, Margaret. "The Marriage Feast." America, 27 October 1973, p. 313.

949. "The Marriage Feast." Booklist, 1 December 1973, p. 369.

950. "The Marriage Feast." Choice 11 (March, 1974), 98.
The reviewer states that, with few exceptions, this volume is identical to the earlier edition of The Eternal Smile. This is not considered a totally new work.

951. Scott, R. E. "The Marriage Feast." Library Journal, 1 December 1973, p. 3578.

Pilgrim at Sea

952. Adams, Phoebe. "Pilgrim at Sea." Atlantic Monthly 213 (March, 1964), 187.

953. Fuller, Edmund. "Pilgrim at Sea." New York Times Book Review, 8 March 1964, p. 34.

954. Fuller, John. "Pilgrim at Sea." New Statesman, 7 February 1964, p. 220.

955. Garrett, T. "Pilgrim at Sea." Best Sellers, 1 March 1964, p. 415.

956. Lindgren, R. E. "Pilgrim at Sea." Library Journal, 15 February 1964, p. 882.

957. Lundbergh, Holger. "Pilgrim at Sea." Saturday Review, 22 February 1964, p. 60.

958. McDonnell, T. P. "Pilgrim at Sea." Critic 22 (April, 1964), 55.

959. Mauer, Robert. "Pilgrim at Sea." Book Week, 1 March 1964, p. 18.

Mauer recognizes that many readers will not find Lagerkvist and his parables to their liking, but that Pilgrim at Sea is a well-written parable.

960. Murray, Michele. "Pilgrim at Sea." Commonweal, 3 April 1964, p. 59.

961. "Pilgrim at Sea." Christian Century, 26 February 1964, p. 274.

962. "Pilgrim at Sea." Library Journal, 15 April 1964, p. 1882.

963. "Pilgrim at Sea." Time, 21 February 1964, p. 96.

964. "Pilgrim at Sea." The Times (London) Literary Supplement, 6 February 1964, p. 101.

The reviewer is of the opinion that Lagerkvist is too uncertain of his own beliefs to write effective parables. The reviewer says Lagerkvist fails to be relevant to twentieth century readers.

The Sibyl

965. Butz, R. C. "*The Sibyl*." *San Francisco Chronicle*, 9 February 1958, p. 27.

966. Davis, R. G. "*The Sibyl*." *New York Times Book Review*, p. 5.
Davis states that there is more beauty and love in *The Sibyl* than in *Barabbas*, but the religious paradoxes remain.

967. Deasy, Philip. "*The Sibyl*." *Commonweal*, 24 January 1958, p. 435.

968. Engle, Paul. "*The Sibyl*." *Chicago Sunday Tribune*, 19 January 1958, p. 7.

969. Hodgart, Patricia. "*The Sibyl*." *Manchester Guardian*, 11 February 1958, p. 4.

970. Libaire, B. B. "*The Sibyl*." *Library Journal*, 15 January 1958, p. 201.

971. Peterson, Virgilia. "*The Sibyl*." *New York Herald-Tribune Book Review*, 2 February 1958, p. 3.

972. Raven, Simon. "*The Sibyl*." *Spectator*, 21 February 1958, p. 238.
Raven says that the book is well-wrought, but that it is blasphemous against man and that its religious sense is masochistic.

973. Rolo, C. J. "*The Sibyl*." *Atlantic Monthly* 201 (February, 1958), 86.

974. "*The Sibyl*." *Booklist*, 15 January 1958, p. 278.

975. "*The Sibyl*." *Kirkus*, 1 December 1957, p. 867.
The reviewer has high praise for *The Sibyl* and also for Naomi Walford's translation.

976. "The Sibyl." Time, 20 January 1958, p. 94.

977. "The Sibyl." The Times (London) Literary Supplement, 31 January 1958, p. 57.

978. Vowles, R. B. "The Sibyl." Saturday Review, 11 January 1958, p. 14.

979. West, Anthony. "The Sibyl." New Yorker, 22 February 1958, p. 135.

VILHELM MOBERG
1898-1973

Vilhelm Moberg was born in the province of Småland, Sweden, on August 20, 1898. Of his childhood he said, "I was born in a soldier's cottage as the fourth child out of seven. My father was a soldier, my grandfather had been a soldier and as long as I can remember there had been soldiers in my family. Soldiering then was socially well considered, but I soon noticed that life for farmers at that time was hard in Sweden, that the struggle for food was a struggle between life and death."[1]

He was born into the peasant community and wrote primarily about peasants and farmers. As he stated, his life was difficult. Industrialization, which was then becoming evident in the region, was creating not only technological, but social, crises. It represented a profound change in the lives of the simple people. Moberg felt a calling to writing instead of farming and so turned to journalism. The theme of the displacement of the peasant recurs in his works.

Like so many Scandinavians, Moberg paid close attention to the words of his elders. His grandmother would tell him stories of her childhood and life as it once was. He acknowledged the influence of his grandmother in his decision to make a career out of writing. Her stories helped him to recognize the terrible plight of the agrarian class and to resolve to try to alleviate its problems. He stated that he dreamed of being a writer, but did not think the dream would come true.

His writing career began in Sweden with the publication of Raskens in 1927. It is the story of a young farmer turned soldier who married a peasant girl and settled on a farm. It is most noteworthy as a piece of history, relating the story of many young Swedish men. In two novels that followed Moberg updated his material somewhat. In those novels he depicted the seductive lure of the city and its effects on farm life. The heroes of those novels refuse to compromise their principles and to yield to the apparent fate of the agrarian community.

Moberg's first international success dealt with much the same theme. The Knut Toring trilogy—Sänkt sedebetyg, Sömnlös, and Giv oss jörden—were published in one volume in English as The Earth Is Ours in 1940. In this he wrote of a successful journalist who realizes that the city is an empty dream and who returns to the land. Near the end of the work it becomes apparent that Moberg saw that faith in the land is not sufficient and his militant anti-Nazi sentiment began to surface.

His firm resistence to Nazism soon became more evident and he displayed contempt for his own country's neutrality in the Second World War. In 1941 he wrote Ride This Night! (published in English in 1943) which deals, on the surface, with a peasant uprising against oppressive German overlords in seventeenth-century Småland. Moberg said, "As writing has always been my way of expressing my feelings, I started the book, Ride This Night!, with its conflict between power and right; its message to those of any century who are murdered and tortured by their dictators was: 'The fiery cross is out. Ride This Night!' The book was published in 1941. Of course the book's meaning was clear to the Nazi regime and accordingly it was confiscated—this I regard as the greatest reward I ever got for any book."

Moberg's greatest success was his emigrant saga. The theme of emigration of Scandinavians to America was a strong and common theme among Swedish and Norwegian writers of this century and the last. The Emigrants, Unto a Good Land, and The Last Letter Home are novels that depict the motives for emigrating and the experience of the characters throughout the process of moving and settling. They are Moberg's attempt to portray the typical emigrant of the nineteenth century.

The writing of those novels began with a question Moberg asked himself: what happened to those who emigrated? He began his research with letters and parish registers and from that the saga grew. He began work twelve years before The Emigrants was published. He traveled to the United States and there studied diaries and other family records.

One criticism of the epic was that Moberg idealized the conditions in America in the nineteenth century. An answer to that criticism came in 1963 in the form of his novel A Time on Earth. In it an old Swedish immigrant in California reminisced. Through the old man Moberg pointed out the poverty and emptiness of life in Småland. Next to it, life in California seemed ideally comfortable.

His novels have a primitive quality with extremely close attention paid to detail. Moberg died in a drowning accident on August, 1973, near Stockholm. At the time of his death he was working on a history of the peasant class of Sweden. The first two volumes of the history have been translated into English by Paul Britten Auten.

NOTE

1 Moberg's comments are from his book, Berättelser ur min levnad (Stockholm: Bonnier, 1968), and are quoted in English in John Wakeman, ed., World Authors, 1950-1970 (New York: H. W. Wilson, 1975), 1007.

MAJOR WORKS IN ENGLISH

The Earth Is Ours. Trans. by Edwin Bjorkman. New York: Simon & Schuster, 1940.

The Emigrants. Trans. by Gustaf Lannestock. New York: Simon & Schuster, 1951.

The Last Letter Home. Trans. by Gustaf Lannestock. New York: Simon & Schuster, 1961.

Memory of Youth. Trans. by Edwin Bjorkman. New York: Simon & Schuster, 1937.

Ride This Night! Trans. by Henry Alexander. Garden City, N. Y.: Doubleday, 1943.

A Time on Earth. Trans. by Naomi Walford. New York: Simon & Schuster, 1965.

Unto a Good Land. Trans. by Gustaf Lannestock. New York: Simon & Schuster, 1954.

When I Was a Child. Trans. by Gustaf Lannestock. New York: Knopf, 1956.

DISSERTATIONS

980. McKnight, Roger Earl. "Moberg's Immigrant Novels and the 'Journals' of Andrew Peterson: A Study of Influences and Parallels." Diss. University of Minnesota, 1974.

981. Thorstensson, Roland B. T. "Vilhelm Moberg as a Dramatist for the People." Diss. University of Washington, 1974.

982. Wright, Rochelle Ann. "Vilhelm Moberg's Image of America." Diss. University of Washington, 1975.

CHAPTERS AND MATERIALS IN BOOKS

983. Bredsdorff, Elias, Brita Mortensen, and Ronald Popperwell, eds. "Swedish Literature, 1870-1950." In An Introduction to Scandinavian Literature from Earliest Times to Our Day. Cambridge: Cambridge University Press, 1951, p. 205.

984. Linner, Sven. "The Hero in Swedish Fiction after World War II." In The Hero in Scandinavian Literature. Ed. John M. Weinstock and Robert T. Rovinsky. Austin, Tex.: University of Texas Press, 1975, pp. 11-2.

985. Robb, Kenneth A. "A Swedish Immigrant in the Land of Oranges." In Essays on California Writers. Ed. Charles L. Crow. Bowling Green, Ky.: Bowling Green University Press, 1978, pp. 79-87.

CRITICAL ARTICLES

986. Alexis, Gerhard T. "Moberg's Immigrant Trilogy: A Dubious Conclusion." Scandinavian Studies 38 (February, 1966), 20-5.

Alexis notes that, while some editing of Moberg's trilogy may have been necessary in the process of translation, the publishers did a disservice to Moberg in the English abridgement of his work.

987. ________. "Vilhelm Moberg: You Can Go Home Again." Scandinavian Studies 40 (August, 1968), 225-32.

Alexis writes that Moberg repeatedly attempts to recapture his own youth in many of his novels. He says that the theme becomes "ineffectual through overuse."

988. ________. "Sweden to Minnesota: Vilhelm Moberg's Fictional Reconstruction." American Quarterly 18 (Spring, 1966), 81-94.

Alexis discusses the American reception of Moberg's trilogy and some of the scholarship spawned by it. He also looks at the historical events that prompted Moberg to write the trilogy.

989. Eiderall, Gunnar. "The Swedes in Moberg's Trilogy." Swedish Pioneer Historical Quarterly 39 (1978), 69-78.

990. Elmen, Paul. "Religious Motifs in The Emigrants." Swedish Pioneer Historical Quarterly 24 (1973), 139-45.

991. Gustafson, Alrik. "Dream Worth Dying for--" American-Scandinavian Review 30 (December, 1942), 296-307.

992. Johnson, Walter. "Moberg's Emigrants and the Naturalistic Tradition." Scandinavian Studies 25 (November, 1953), 134-46.

993. Orton, Gavin and Philip Holmes. "Memoirs of an Idealist: Vilhelm Moberg's Soddat med brutet gevär." Scandinavian Studies 48 (Winter, 1976), 29-51.
Orton and Holmes study Soldat med brutet gevär as a Bildungsroman, as a social history of Sweden during the early part of this century, as an attack on the Social Democrats for the betrayal of their ideals, and as an autobiographical novel.

994. Paul, R. "Vilhelm Moberg and Swedish Arbetarlitteratur." History Workshop 4 (1977), 226-7.

995. Winther, Sophus Keith. "Moberg and a New Genre for the Emigrant Novel." Scandinavian Studies 34 (August, 1962), 170-82.
Winther acknowledges the criticism of looseness of structure of Moberg's emigrant trilogy (particularly with regard to Unto a Good Land), but he praises the portrayal of the people who emigrated from Sweden to America.

996. Wright, R. "Vilhelm Moberg in America." Scandinavian Studies 51 (Winter, 1979), 99-101.

BOOK REVIEWS

The Earth Is Ours

997. "The Earth Is Ours." New Republic, 14 April 1941, p. 510.

998. "The Earth Is Ours." New Yorker, 22 March 1941, p. 84.

999. "The Earth Is Ours." Springfield Republican, 6 April 1941, p. 7e.

1000. "The Earth Is Ours." Time, 31 March 1941, p. 75.

1001. Hansen, A. C. "The Earth Is Ours." Library Journal, 15 February 1941, p. 178.

1002. Hauser, Marianne. "The Earth Is Ours." New York Times Book Review, 23 March 1941, p. 8.
Hauser says that Moberg is occasionally prone to "slow or overconscientious moods," but the book is full of life and subtlety.

1003. Mann, D. L. "The Earth Is Ours." Boston Transcript, 22 March 1941, p. 2.
Mann states that the importance of the novel lies in the changes portrayed in the peasant class. He says it is a hopeful book.

1004. Rugoff, Milton. "The Earth Is Ours." New York Herald-Tribune Books, 23 March 1941, p. 7.

The Emigrants

1005. Aldridge, Jack. "The Emigrants." San Francisco Chronicle, 29 July 1951, p. 14.

1006. Butcher, Fanny. "The Emigrants." Chicago Sunday Tribune, 15 July 1951, p. 3.

1007. Chapin, Ruth. "The Emigrants." Christian Science Monitor, 19 July 1951, p. 7.

1008. "The Emigrants." Booklist, 1 September 1951, p. 12.

1009. "The Emigrants." Bookmark 11 (November, 1951), 34.

1010. "The Emigrants." Kirkus, 1 March 1951, p. 135.

1011. "The Emigrants." New Yorker, 28 July 1951, p. 75.

1012. Hughes, Riley. "The Emigrants." Catholic World 175 (October, 1951), 73.

1013. McKay, M. P. "The Emigrants." Library Journal, 15 June 1951, p. 1027.

1014. Nerber, John. "The Emigrants." New York Times Book Review, 15 July 1951, p. 5.
Nerber is impressed with the detail of The Emigrants. He also notes the range of emotions and human traits in the novel.

1015. Smith, Harrison. "The Emigrants." Saturday Review of Literature, 28 July 1951, p. 11.
Smith says that the documentation of Moberg does not make the book easy to read, but it is one of the soundest and most inspiring novels to appear in 1951.

1016. Strode, Hudson. "The Emigrants." New York Herald-Tribune Books, 15 July 1951, p. 4.
Strode praises Moberg's clarity and use of irony. He says that the earthiness may be a bit much for some readers.

The Last Letter Home

1017. Haas, V. P. "The Last Letter Home." New York Times Book Review, 2 July 1961, p. 6.
Haas finds Moberg's prose style at time reminiscent of the Bible. He also praises Lannestock's translation.

1018. "The Last Letter Home." Booklist, 15 July 1961, p. 695.

1019. "The Last Letter Home." Kirkus, 1 April 1961, p. 345.

1020. "The Last Letter Home." Kliatt Paperback Book Guide, 13 (Spring, 1979), 10.

1021. "The Last Letter Home." New Yorker, 24 June 1961, p. 95.

1022. "The Last Letter Home." Springfield Republican, 9 July 1961, p. 5D.

1023. "The Last Letter Home." The Times (London) Literary Supplement, 27 October 1961, p. 777.

1024. Lindgren, R. E. "The Last Letter Home." Library Journal 86 (July, 1961), 2492.

1025. Siebel, Julian. "The Last Letter Home." Chicago Sunday Tribune, 25 June 1961, p. 3.

1026. Walsh, Chad. "The Last Letter Home." New York Herald-Tribune Books, 30 July 1961, p. 11.
Walsh states that the characterizations are skillfully crafted and that the book is well-written, neither strident nor sensational.

Memory of Youth

1027. Geismar, Maxwell. "Memory of Youth." New York Herald-Tribune Books, 3 April 1938, p. 23.

1028. Hutchison, Percy. "Memory of Youth." New York Times Book Review, 10 April 1938, p. 5.

1029. MacAfee, Helen. "Memory of Youth." Yale Review n. s. 27 (Summer, 1938), vi.

1030. "Memory of Youth." Christian Science Monitor, 27 July 1938, p. 10.
The reviewer says that the writing is not outstanding, the main character is uninteresting, the theme is common, and the novel is not very substantial.

1031. "Memory of Youth." New Republic, 20 April 1938, p. 342.

1032. "Memory of Youth." Saturday Review of Literature, 30 April 1938, p. 20.
This reviewer is of the opinion that the book is well-written and will win esteem for Moberg. Bjorkman's translation is also praised.

1033. "Memory of Youth." Springfield Republican, 15 May 1938, p. 7e.

1034. "Memory of Youth." Time, 18 April 1938, p. 83.

Ride This Night!

1035. Bernt, H. H. A. "Ride This Night!" Library Journal, 15 May 1943, p. 430.

1036. Gorman, Robert. "Ride This Night!" New Republic, 5 July 1943, p. 28.

1037. "Ride This Night!" Booklist, 15 July, 1943, p. 464.

1038. "Ride This Night!" Commonweal, 11 June 1943, p. 204.

1039. "Ride This Night!" New Yorker, 5 June 1943, p. 85.
The reviewer says the narrative is superior to most historical novels, but doesn't believe the hero becomes a symbol of revolt.

1040. Sapieha, Virgilia. "Ride This Night!" New York Herald-Tribune Books, 23 May 1943, p. 4.

1041. Toksvig, Signe. "Ride This Night!" New York Times Book Review, 23 May 1943, p. 6.

1042. Trilling, Diana. "Ride This Night!" Nation, 12 June 1943, p. 843.
Trilling is fond of the folklore that is included in the novel which, she says, salvages the "Knut Hamsunish bread-and-water, ox-and-plow rhythm of his prose."

The Settlers

1043. "The Settlers." Booklist, 1 January 1979, p. 734.

A Time on Earth

1044. Burgess, E. "A Time on Earth." Punch, 1 September 1965, p. 326.

1045. Engle, Paul. "A Time on Earth." New York Times Book Review, 1 August 1965, p. 27.
Engle notes an atmosphere of gloom surrounding the main character, Albert Carlson, but he says that Moberg has the ability to effectively contrast past and present.

1046. Harrison, K. "A Time on Earth." Spectator, 13 August 1965, p. 213.

1047. Hattman, John. "A Time on Earth." Best Sellers, 15 July 1965, p. 177.
Hattman praises the book as being "well-plotted" and "well-developed." He also says it is of high literary merit, but that it might be best suited to the "mature and discriminating adult."

1048. Johnson, W. S. "A Time on Earth." Saturday Review, 10 July 1965, p. 42.

1049. Lindahl, L. "A Time on Earth." Books Abroad 38 (Summer, 1965), 347.

1050. Lindgren, R. E. "A Time on Earth." Library Journal 90 (July, 1965), 3073.

1051. "A Time on Earth." Booklist, 1 September 1965, p. 43.

1052. "A Time on Earth." Choice 2 (January, 1966), 778.

1053. "A Time on Earth." Kirkus, 1 May 1965, p. 482.

1054. "A Time on Earth." New Yorker, 17 July 1965, p. 108.

1055. "A Time on Earth." Observer (London), 8 August 1965, p. 21.

1056. "A Time on Earth." The Times (London) Literary Supplement, 12 August 1965, p. 693.

Unto a Good Land

1057. Barrett, Mary. "Unto a Good Land." Library Journal 79 (July, 1954), 1310.

Barrett praises Moberg's imaginative powers, remarking on the fact that he had never been to America. He gained his knowledge from reading and from some relatives' accounts.

1058. Butcher, Fanny. "Unto a Good Land." Chicago Sunday Tribune, 1 August 1954, p. 3.

Butcher calls the novel "a masterpiece of understatement." She is especially impressed by the factual detail of the emigration.

1059. Haas, V. P. "Unto a Good Land." New York Times Book Review, 1 August 1954, p. 5.

Haas says that Moberg's "style is ponderous, his prose phlegmatic, his imagination pedestrian," but he finds many things to recommend the book.

1060. Hughes, Riley. "Unto a Good Land." Catholic World 180 (October, 1954), 72.

1061. Peterson, Virgilia. "Unto a Good Land." New York Herald-Tribune Books, 1 August 1954, p. 3.

1062. Pisko, E. S. "Unto a Good Land." Christian Science Monitor, 5 August 1954, p. 11.

1063. "Unto a Good Land." Booklist, 15 July 1954, p. 452.

1064. "Unto a Good Land." Cleveland Open Shelf, September 1954, p. 32.

1065. "Unto a Good Land." Kirkus, 15 May 1954, p. 320.

1066. "Unto a Good Land." New Yorker, 14 August 1954, p. 82.

1067. "Unto a Good Land." Springfield Republican, 29 August 1954, p. 6C.

1068. "Unto a Good Land." Wisconsin Library Bulletin 50 (October, 1954), 211.

1069. Vowles, R. B. "Unto a Good Land." Saturday Review, 31 July 1954, p. 12.

When I Was a Child

1070. Barker, G. A. "When I Was a Child." San Francisco Chronicle, 22 April 1956, p. 21.

1071. Gray, James. "When I Was a Child." Chicago Sunday Tribune, 22 April 1956, p. 3.

Gray is impressed by the depiction of local tradition and the passion and humor of the novel. He also notes the development of the mind of the boy.

1072. Haas, V. P. "When I Was a Child." New York Times Book Review, 18 March 1956, p. 4.

Haas states that the novel is at times a bit ponderous, but it is absorbing and intense. He also praises Lannestock's translation.

1073. Libaire, B. B. "When I Was a Child." Library Journal, 15 March 1956, p. 716.

1074. Lillard, R. G. "When I Was a Child." New York Herald-Tribune Books, 18 March 1956, p. 1.

1075. Mansten, S. P. "When I Was a Child." Saturday Review, 7 April 1956, p. 28.

1076. "When I Was a Child." Booklist, 15 April 1956, p. 340.

1077. "When I Was a Child." Bookmark 15 (April, 1956), 161.

1078. "When I Was a Child." Canadian Forum 36 (September, 1956), 143.

The reviewer notes that readers may find similarities between life in Sweden and other pioneer tales, but the larger issues dealt with make it a superior book.

1079. "When I Was a Child." Kirkus, 1 February 1956, p. 93.

1080. "When I Was a Child." Wisconsin Library Bulletin 52 (May, 1956), 125.

HALLDÓR LAXNESS
1902-

Born Halldór Guðjónsson on April 23, 1902, in Reykjavik, Iceland, Halldór soon took the name Laxness, after the name of the farm to which his family moved in 1905. As a result of the move, Halldór spent most of his young life in the country. Like other Scandinavian writers, Halldór learned a great deal by listening to a member of the older generation. His grandmother would sing age-old songs to him and tell of the Iceland of the Middle Ages. Laxness said that she lived more in the eighteenth century than the twentieth and found many new ideas and inventions impossible to accept.

Laxness also said that he disliked the daily chores on the farm and tried continuously to avoid them. As a young boy, even as early as the age of seven, he felt a calling to the literary life. He jotted down thoughts and youthful stories and poems at every opportunity. As he went about his daily work he kept a notebook with him to write whenever time permitted.

He found the traditional school system to be boring and stifling. Just after his father's death in 1919 he decided that he had had enough of school. He traveled to Denmark that summer. By that time he had already written a short novel that was published in Reykjavik in the autumn. It displayed little of his mature talent, but was an important accomplishment for a seventeen-year-old boy. Several critics have stated that the novel owed quite a lot to Hamsun and Lagerlöf, particularly in its glorification of the working of the soil.

In 1921 and 1922 Laxness again traveled to Europe, this time primarily to Germany and Austria. He was later received as a guest of the Benedictine monastery of Saint Maurice de Clervaux in Luxembourg. He was soon baptized and confirmed in the Catholic faith. At the time he was received into the church he planned to devote his life to the Catholic church. He stated in letters that he intended to study in Rome and eventually be ordained into the priesthood. He never began his theological studies, though, and, after a few years, left the church entirely.

After Laxness met with some literary success in his native Iceland, he made the decision to enlarge the scope of his writing and his audience. Since he had already traveled in Europe, it was logical that America was his next stop. So, in the summer of 1927 he arrived in America and stayed until the end of 1929. He spent most of the two-and-a-half years in southern California. There he became acquainted with Upton Sinclair, wrote movie scripts (though none were ever produced), and lectured extensively. Those experiences caused him to mature greatly as a writer.

After his return to Iceland Laxness published some poetry and the novel *Salka Valka*, the first drafts of which were written in America. Salka Valka, the main character of the book, is probably the most fully developed female character Laxness ever created. It is, to a great degree, a social novel that is satiric of the political and social climate of Iceland. In fact, there is much astute contemporary commentary in the novel. It has frequently been noted that in writing the novel Laxness was influenced by Dickens, in the satire of social conditions and in the desire for social justice.

In 1934 and 1935 Laxness published *Independent People* in two volumes. That novel centers around the small farmer and his plight. Because of its subject matter it was often compared to Knut Hamsun's *Growth of the Soil*. About the comparison Laxness said in a postscript to the second Icelandic edition of *Independent People*:

> I do not wish to claim that all of the social—or other—conclusions in *Sjalfstaett fólk* [*Independent People*] are the right ones, but my certainty that Hamsun's social conclusions in *Markens Gröde* [*Growth of the Soil*] were on the whole erroneous had its part to play in the origin of my book. These two books, like thousands of other

> books, have in common the fact that they deal with farmers and their problems; but the keynote of the one book is clearly opposed to that of the other.

The interesting question of Independent People is how a man of cunning, strong will, and endurance could fail in the attempt to provide for himself and his family. In asking the question, Laxness portrayed the mechanistic forces of society.

Laxness admired the clarity of Hemingway's prose and the sharp definition of his characters. So much did he admire him that he translated A Farewell to Arms into Icelandic in 1941. To Laxness, Hemingway's style most perfectly illustrated the spirit of the times. Laxness also found a similarity between Hemingway's style of writing and that of the ancient Icelandic sagas. In Laxness's translation of the sagas he noted and adapted Hemingway's narrative technique and character portrayal. He adapted aspects of Hemingway's style in his own novel, Islandsklukkan, which has not been translated.

In 1955 Halldór Laxness was awarded the Nobel Prize in literature. Although the award was bestowed upon him at a relatively early age (fifty-three years old), Laxness continued writing at a high level of productivity. He has continued to write and has published several works, The Fish Can Sing and Paradise Reclaimed notable among them. The

Nobel Prize allowed Laxness to travel extensively to lands he had not previously visited, including China, India, and Israel.

He has of late turned his pen more to social matters. His social criticism has led him to be skeptical of all rigid ideologies and to concentrate more on the results of the social system. Thus, he had some praise for Maoist China and its ability to feed and to assure the employ of its people. He denounced the Soviet system of socialism and the jargonistic attempts to cover up its deficiencies. He continues to see the artist as a source of creation in a world still in the process of being created. If other forces tend toward the destructive, art is responsible for creation nevertheless. This has been Laxness's most enduring belief.

MAJOR WORKS IN ENGLISH

The Fish Can Sing. Trans. by Magnus Magnusson. New York: Crowell, 1967.

Independent People. Trans. by J. A. Thompson. New York: Knopf, 1946.

Paradise Reclaimed. Trans. by Magnus Magnusson. New York: Crowell, 1962.

Salka Valka. Trans. by F. H. Lyon. Boston: Houghton Mifflin, 1936.

BOOKS

1081. Hallberg, Peter. Halldór Laxness. Trans. Rory McTurk. New York: Twayne, 1971.

Hallberg spends a little time in his biography of Laxness relating the background of the Icelandic writer, including Laxness' attempts at reconciling his Christianity with his social radicalism. Much of Hallberg's book is an analysis of Laxness' writings. Hallberg also studies the effects of the Nobel Prize on Laxness' later writing and on the perception of his writing.

THESES

1082. Markey, Thomas L. "Background and Aspects of Halldór Laxness' Salka Valka." Master's Thesis. University of Chicago, 1965.

CHAPTERS AND MATERIALS IN BOOKS

1083. Bach, Giovanni. "Icelandic Literature." In A History of the Scandinavian Literatures. Trans. and ed. Frederika Blankner. New York: Dial, 1938, pp. 270-1.

1084. Einarsson, Stefan. "Halldór(Gudjonsson) Kiljan Laxness." In History of Icelandic Prose Writers, 1800-1940. Cornell: Cornell University Press, 1948, pp. 219-29.

In this sketch, Einarsson focuses on some of the major influences on Laxness' writings. These include his theological training, Communism, and other writers, notably Ernest Hemingway.

1085. Einarsson, Stefan. "Halldór Kiljan Laxness." In _A History of Icelandic Literature_. New York: The Johns Hopkins Press for the American-Scandinavian Foundation, 1957, pp. 317-9.
Einarsson presents a brief sketch of the creative life of Laxness.

1086. Haugen, Einar. "Laxness and the Americas." In _Afmaeliskvedur heiman og handan: Til Halldors Kiljans Laxness sextugs_. Ed. Ragnar Johnson. Reykjavik: Helgafell, 1962, pp. 44-7.
This and the articles that follow are English articles that appear in Johnson's Icelandic work.

1087. Kozhernikov, Vadin, et. al. "The Powerful Youthful Voice of the Northern Skald." In _Afmaeliskvedur heiman og handan: Til Halldors Kiljans Laxness sextugs_. Ed. Ragnar Johnson. Reykjavik: Helgafell, 1962, pp. 59-60.

1088. MacQueen, John. "Theology and the Atom Station." In _Afmaeliskvedur heiman og handan: Til Halldors Kiljans Laxness sextug_. Ed. Ragnar Johnson. Reykjavik: Helgafell, 1962, pp. 80-3.

1089. Maurer, K. W. "A Tribute from Canada." In _Afmaeliskvedur heiman og handan: Til Halldors Kiljans Laxness sextugs_. Ed. Ragnar Johnson. Reykjavik: Hegafell, 1962, pp. 84-8.

1090. Morgan, Edwin. "The Atom Station and the Degrees of Realism." In _Afmaeliskvedur heiman og handan: Til Halldors Kiljans Laxness sextugs_. Ed. Ragnar Johnson. Reykjavik: Helgafell, 1962, pp. 89-93.

1091. Venclora, Antasas. "Halldór Laxness." In _Afmaeliskvedur heiman og handan: Til Halldors Kiljans Laxness sextugs_, Ed. Ragnar Johnson. Reykjavik: Helgafell, 1962, pp. 117-8.

CRITICAL ARTICLES

1092. Beck, Richard. "The Literary Scene in Iceland." American-Scandinavian Review 34 (March, 1946), 56-60.

1093. Dorsteinsson, Steingrimur J. "Halldór Laxness and the Icelandic Sagas." Scandinavica 11 (May, 1972), 101-16.
Dorsteinsson treats Laxness as a kind of documentary novelist, a chronicler of his land and of his people.

1094. Einarsson, Stefan. "A Contemporary Icelandic Author." Life and Letters 14 (Summer, 1936), 24-30.

1095. ________. "Five Icelandic Novelists." Books Abroad 16 (July, 1942), 254-9.

1096. Hallberg, Peter. "The Dialogue in Islandsklukkan." Scandinavica 11 (May, 1972), sup., 33-44.
Hallberg sees the dialogue in Islandsklukkan as more than a means of communication between characters. He views the speakers as representatives of the Icelandic nation and its history.

1097. Haugen, Einar. "Thalia in Reykjavik." American-Scandinavian Review 44 (December, 1956), 335-40.

1098. Herring, Robert. "Review of Salka Valka." Life and Letters 14 (Summer, 1936), 185-90.

1099. "The Icelandic Microcosm." The Times (London) Literary Supplement 11 September 1969, 1001-2.

1100. Jacobs, Fred R. "Halldór Laxness and America: A Bibliography." Serif 10 (Winter, 1973), 24-34.

1101. Johannessen, Matthias. "Talking to Laxness." Trans. Alan Boucher. Atlantica and Iceland Review 10, iii (1972), 26-9, 31.

1102. Johnsen, Arni. "*The Fish Can Sing*: Old Iceland Revived on the Screen." *Atlantica and Iceland Review* 11, i (1973), 28-35.

1103. Kissane, L. "An American Reader Looks at Laxness." *Atlantica and Iceland Review* 10, ii (1972), 68-9, 71.

1104. McTurk, Rory. "Swift, Laxness, and the Eskimos." *Scandinavica* 11 (May, 1972), sup., 45-62.
In discussing Laxness' *Gerple*, McTurk suggests that Laxness wrote with Swift in mind. He parallels Laxness' depiction of Eskimos with parts of *Gulliver's Travels*.

1105. Magnusson, Sigurdur A. "A Bird's-eye View of Icelandic Literature." *Iceland Review* 1 (August-September, 1963), 11-2.

1106. ________. "Halldór Kiljan Laxness." *American-Scandinavian Review* 4 (March, 1956), 13-8.

1107. ________. "Laxness Reviews His Past." *Iceland Review* 2, i (1964), 11-2.

1108. ________. "The Presser and the Pigeons." *Iceland Review* 4, iii (1966), 21-5, 27.

1109. Markey, Thomas L. "'Salka Valka': A Study in Social Realism." *Scandinavica* 11 (May, 1972), sup., 63-9.
Markey refers to *Salka Valka* as a collectivist novel, a product of an age of socialism. Markey cites Dreiser, Lewis, and Sinclair as having the most pronounced influence on Laxness in the sphere of collectivism.

1110. ________. "*Sjálfstaett Fólk*, Hamsun, and Rousseau." *Edda* 54, v (1967), 346-58.

1111. Nedelyaeva-Steponavichiene, Svetlana. "On the Style of Laxness' Tetralogy: 'World Light'." *Scandinavica* 11 (May, 1972), sup., 71-87.
Nedelyaeva-Steponavichiene views the style of *World Light* as objective and realistic, opposed to and perhaps at war with a subjective, romantic style.

1112. Ringler, Richard N. "Christianity on the Slopes of the Glacier." Books Abroad 44 (1974), 54-5.

1113. Sørensen, Preben Meulengracht. "Being Faithful to Oneself." Scandinavica 11 (May, 1972), sup., 89-100.

Sørensen sees the national theme as secondary to a myth about the greatness of man in some of Laxness' works. Sørensen also notes some similarities between Laxness and his narrators.

1114. Sorrell, Mary. "Halldór Kiljan Laxness: The Icelandic Epic Novelist." Apollo 43 (February, 1956), 64-5.

1115. Tate, G. S. "Laxness, Halldor, Mormons and Promised Land." Dialogue: A Journal of Mormon Thought 11 (1978), 25-37.

1116. Thompson, Lawrence S. "Halldór Kiljan Laxness." Books Abroad 28 (Summer, 1954), 298-9.

1117. "Writer in a Small Language Community." The Times (London) Literary Supplement, 25 September 1969, 1057-9.

BOOK REVIEWS

The Fish Can Sing

1118. Adams, Phoebe. "The Fish Can Sing." Atlantic Monthly 219 (April, 1967), 150.

Adams sees Laxness' style as a throwback to Icelandic sagas. She says this style involves understatement, which some readers may not care for.

1119. Bannon, B. A. "The Fish Can Sing." Publishers Weekly, 16 January 1967, p. 31.

1120. "*The Fish Can Sing*." *Booklist*, 1 April 1967, p. 837.

1121. "*The Fish Can Sing*." *Time*, 14 April 1967, p. 118.

1122. "*The Fish Can Sing*." *The Times (London) Literary Supplement*, 3 November 1966, p. 997.
The reviewer finds the comic scenes engaging, but the descriptive passages dull. Laxness' attempts to portray the virtue of some of the characters slow the novel down.

1123. Jacobs, Barry. "*The Fish Can Sing*." *Saturday Review*, 27 May 1967, p. 31.

1124. Linehan, E. J. "*The Fish Can Sing*." *Best Sellers*, 1 April 1967, p. 8.

1125. Morgan, Edwin. "*The Fish Can Sing*." *New Statesman*, 30 September 1967, p. 486.

Independent People

1126. Basso, Hamilton. "*Independent People*." *New Yorker*, 19 August 1946, p. 88.
Basso finds the novel long and slow-moving. He finds *Independent People* somewhat impressive, particularly its bulk.

1127. Butterfield, Roger. "*Independent People*." *Saturday Review of Literature*, 27 July 1946, p. 12.

1128. Davis, R. G. "*Independent People*." *New York Times Book Review*, 28 July 1946, p. 1.

1129. Etzkorn, L. R. "*Independent People*." *Library Journal* 71 (July, 1946), 978.

1130. Evans, Ernestine. "Independent People." New York Herald-Tribune Books, 28 July 1946, p. 3.
Evans sees the book as being relevant in all times. She says it is bold, moving, and thought-provoking, and that the reader sees Iceland before religions from the East or the West reached it.

1131. "Independent People." Booklist, 1 October 1946, p. 36.

1132. "Independent People." Bookmark 7 (November, 1946), 13.

1133. "Independent People." Christian Science Monitor, 9 August 1946, p. 14.

1134. "Independent People." Kirkus, 15 March 1946, p. 130.
This reviewer calls the book "bleak and bitter" and says that it is too long and too somber.

1135. "Independent People." New Republic, 23 September 1946, p. 357.

1136. "Independent People." Time, 5 August 1946, p. 102.

1137. Lancaster, Bruce. "Independent People." Atlantic Monthly 178 (September, 1946), 150.

1138. Levene, Carol. "Independent People." San Francisco Chronicle, 4 August 1946, p. 14.

1139. North, Sterling. "Independent People." Chicago Sun Book Week, 28 July 1946, p. 2.

1140. Prescott, Orville. "Independent People." Yale Review n. s. (Autumn, 1946), 190.

1141. Sloane, T. O. "Independent People." Commonweal, 30 August 1946, p. 482.

Paradise Reclaimed

1142. Barrett, William. "Paradise Reclaimed." Atlantic Monthly 210 (December, 1962), 172.
Barrett finds Steinor a beguiling character. He also notes the qualities of the saga evident in Laxness' writing.

1143. Devan, Richard. "Paradise Reclaimed." Library Journal, 15 December 1962, p. 4559.

1144. "Paradise Reclaimed." New Yorker, 9 February 1963, p. 142.

1145. "Paradise Reclaimed." Time, 23 November 1962, p. 83.

1146. Perkin, R. L. "Paradise Reclaimed." Saturday Review, 2 February 1963, p. 40.

1147. Sorensen, Virginia. "Paradise Reclaimed." New York Times Book Review, 18 November 1962, p. 67.
Sorensen notes that the novel is clearly and completely Scandinavian, particularly in the mixture of reality and magic.

1148. Spector, Robert Donald. "Paradise Reclaimed." New York Herald-Tribune Books, 18 November 1962, p. 6.

Salka Valka

1149. Carleton, P. D. "Salka Valka." Saturday Review of Literature, 23 May 1936, p. 12.

1150. Einarsson, Stefan. "Salka Valka." Boston Transcript, 2 May 1936, p. 1.

1151. Kazin, Alfred. "Salka Valka." New York Herald-Tribune Books, 3 May 1936, p. 9.
Kazin finds much impressive about Salka Valka, but he says that the translation is awkward, since it was translated into English from a Danish translation of the original Icelandic.

1152. Plomer, William. "Salka Valka." Spectator, 28 February 1936, p. 366.

1153. "Salka Valka." Manchester Guardian, 21 Febraury 1936, p. 7.

1154. "Salka Valka." Springfield Republican, 7 June 1936, p. 7e.

1155. "Salka Valka." Time, 18 May 1936, p. 86.

1156. "Salka Valka." The Times (London) Literary Supplement, 8 February 1936, p. 113.
The reviewer states that the novel is sharp and vivid despite difficulties in attempts to reconcile Christian doctrines with more modern ideologies, such as Communism.

1157. Schnell, Jonathan. "Salka Valka." Forum 96 (July, 1936), vi.

1158. Swinnerton, Frank. "Salka Valka." Chicago Daily Tribune, 7 March 1936, p. 12.

1159. Vaughn, Richard. "Salka Valka." New Republic, 24 June 1936, p. 219.

1160. Young, Stanley. "Salka Valka." New York Times Book Review, 18 May 1936, p. 7.
Laxness's portrayal of a vigorous woman is particularly striking to Young. He does not find it as penetrating as Undset's characterizations, but he says that it is original.

World Light

1161. Thompson, Lawrence S. "World Light." Library Journal 94 (July, 1969), 2640.

1162. "World Light." Booklist, 15 July 1969, p. 1259.
The reviewer notes that Magnusson's translation is an effective one. He also notes that the edition is an attempt to familiarize American readers with Laxness.

1163. "World Light." The Times (London) Literary Supplement, 11 September 1969, p. 1001.

INDEX TO AUTHORS, EDITORS, AND TRANSLATORS

The numbers in this index refer to entry numbers, not page numbers.

ABOUT THE COMPILER

John Budd is Instructor and Reference Librarian at Southeastern Louisiana University in Hammond, Louisiana.

www.ingramcontent.com/pod-product-compliance
Lightning Source LLC
Chambersburg PA
CBHW060529310726
48982CB00002B/472

9780313228698